Table of Co

1. Presidential Assassinat

8. Tecumseh's Curse

17. Lincoln Assassination Conspiracies

26. Assassination of James A. Garfield

50. McKinley Assassination

55. Death of JFK

66. Andrew Jackson Survives Attempt

69. Teddy Roosevelt Shot

76. FDR Attempt

84. Truman Assassination Attempt

95. Gerald Ford Attempt

111. Ronald Reagan Attempt

Presidential Assassinations and Assassination Attempts

Assassinations and the American Presidency

In the history of the presidency, four presidents have actually died from assassination. Another six were the subject of assassination attempts. Following is a description of each assassination and attempt.

Assassinations

Abraham Lincoln - Lincoln was shot in the head while watching a play on April 14, 1865. His assassin, John Wilkes Booth escaped and was later shot and killed. Conspirators who helped plan Lincoln's assassination were found guilty and hung. Lincoln died on April 15, 1865.

James Garfield - Charles J. Guiteau, a mentally disturbed government office seeker, shot Garfield on July 2, 1881. The president did not die until September 19th of blood poisoning. This was related more to the manner in which the physicians attended to the president than to the wounds themselves. Guiteau was convicted of murder and hanged on June 30, 1882.

William McKinley - McKinley was shot two times by anarchist Leon Czolgosz while the president was visiting the Pan-American Exhibit in Buffalo, New York on September 6, 1901. He died on September 14, 1901. Czolgosz stated that he shot McKinley because he was an enemy of working people. He was convicted of the murder and electrocuted on October 29, 1901.

John F. Kennedy - On November 22, 1963, John F. Kennedy was mortally wounded

while riding in a motorcade in Dallas, Texas. His apparent assassin, Lee Harvey Oswald, was killed by Jack Ruby before standing trial. The Warren Commission was called to investigate Kennedy's death and found that Oswald had acted alone to kill Kennedy. Many argued, however, that there was more than one gunman, a theory upheld by a 1979 House Committee investigation. The FBI and a 1982 study disagreed. Speculation continues to this day.

Assassination Attempts

Andrew Jackson - On January 30, 1835, Andrew Jackson was attending a funeral for Congressman Warren Davis. Richard Lawrence, attempted to shoot him with two different derringers, each of which misfired. He was tried for the attempted assassination but was found not guilty by reason of insanity. He spent the rest of his life in an insane asylum.

Theodore Roosevelt - An assassination attempt was actually not made on Roosevelt's life while he was in the office of president. Instead, it occurred after he had left office and decided to run for another term against William Howard Taft. While campaigning on October 14, 1912, he was shot in the chest by John Schrank, a mentally disturbed New York saloonkeeper. Luckily, Roosevelt had a speech and his spectacle case in his pocket that slowed down the .38 caliber bullet. The bullet was never removed but allowed to heal over.

Franklin Roosevelt - After giving a speech in Miami on February 15, 1933, Giuseppe Zangara shot six shots into the crowd. None hit Roosevelt though the Mayor of Chicago, Anton Cermak was shot in the stomach. Zangara blamed

wealthy capitalists for his plights and those of other working people. He was convicted of attempted murder and then after Cermak's death due to the shooting he was retried for murder. He was executed by electric chair in March, 1933.

Harry Truman

On November 1, 1950, two Puerto Rican nationals attempted to kill President Truman to bring attention to the case for Puerto Rican independence. The President and his family were staying at the Blair House across from the White House and the two attempted assassins, Oscar Collazo and Griselio Torresola, tried to shoot their way into the house. Torresola killed one and wounded another policeman while Collazo wounded one policeman. Torresola died in the gunfight. Collazo was arrested and sentenced to death which Truman commuted to life in prison. Carter freed Collazo from prison in 1979.

Gerald Ford

Ford escaped two assassination attempts, both by women. First on September 5, 1975, Lynette Fromme, a follower of Charles Manson, pointed a gun at him but did not fire. She was convicted of attempting to assassinate the president and sentenced to life in prison. The second attempt on Ford's life occurred on September 22, 1975 when Sara Jane Moore fired one shot that was deflected by a bystander. Moore was trying to prove herself to some radical friends with the assassination of the president. She was convicted of attempted assassination and sentenced to life in prison.

Ronald Reagan - On March 30, 1981, Reagan was shot in the lung by John Hinckley, Jr. Hinckley hoped that by assassinating the president, he would earn enough notoriety to impress Jodie Foster. He also shot Press Secretary James Brady along with an officer and a security agent. He was arrested but found not guilty by reason of insanity. He was sentenced to life in a mental institution.

One fascinating side note to presidential assassinations and deaths in office is Tecumseh's Curse whereby presidents starting with William Henry Harrison who were elected in a year ending with a zero were assassinated or died while in office. The curse ended with Ronald Reagan.

What is Tecumseh's Curse?

Tecumseh's Curse (a.k.a The Curse of Tippecanoe) is a legend associated with the fact that every president who was elected in a year ending in zero – from William Henry Harrison (1840) to John F. Kennedy (1860) – died in office. Proponents of Tecumseh's Curse refer to the adversarial relationship between Tecumseh (a visionary Native American leader) and William Henry Harrison as the origin of seven presidential deaths.

Tecumseh's Curse Presidents?

Post-Tecumseh's Curse?

Let's take a closer look at the election years and what happened to each president.

1840: William Henry Harrison – *Died* in office of pneumonia
1860: Abraham Lincoln – *Assassinated* by John Wilkes Booth in Ford's Theatre
1880: James A. Garfield – *Assassinated* by Charles Guiteau in a Washington, D.C. train station
1900: William McKinley – *Assassinated* by Leon Czolgosz in Buffalo, New York
1920: Warren G. Harding – *Died* in office,

possibly of ptomaine poisoning that progressed to pneumonia
1940: Franklin D. Roosevelt – *Died* in office of a massive cerebral hemorrhage
1960: John F. Kennedy – *Assassinated* by Lee Harvey Oswald in Dallas, Texas
1980: Ronald Reagan – *Lived* (Shot in the chest by John Warnock Hinckley Jr., but survived – Curse over?)
2000: George W. Bush – *Lived*

The Birth of a Legend

Those who attempt to make sense of these eerie twists of fate have come to blame a Native American curse for historical coincidence. Nevertheless, let's examine Tecumseh's Curse a little closer by looking at the birth of the legend.

Fictionalized painting of Tecumseh in a British uniform – from the late 1800s. No authenticated portrait of Tecumseh exists.

Who was Tecumseh?

Tecumseh was a remarkable Native American leader. Born circa 1768, he was a Shawnee Chief from the Ohio River Valley who envisioned a vast Indian Confederacy to keep the Ohio River as a border between Native Americans and American settlers.

What did Tecumseh do?

Throughout the early 1800s, Tecumseh and his brother Tenskwatawa (The Prophet) traveled extensively among tribes – all the way from Wisconsin to Florida. Tecumseh was an excellent speaker, and he convinced many tribes to join his cause for Native American unity. By 1808, a significant number of Native American warriors gathered under Tecumseh's leadership. Around this time, Tecumseh and Tenskwatawa founded Prophet's Town at the junction of the Wabash and Tippecanoe Rivers, near present-day Lafayette, Indiana. Subsequently, Prophet's Town became the site of a large confederacy of Midwestern and southern tribes – assembled to stop American settlers from spreading into Native American lands.

Painting of William Henry Harrison, c. 1813 – by Rembrandt Peale, National Portrait Gallery

William Henry Harrison confronts Tecumseh's Confederation

William Henry Harrison, Governor of the Indian Territory, was given the task of confronting Tecumseh and his confederacy of warriors. In early November 1811 Harrison organized a group of 1,000 men and arrived outside of Prophet's Town. While Tecumseh was gone to recruit more allies, Tenskwatawa ordered an attack on Harrison and his men. However, the Native American forces under Tenskwatawa were eventually overtaken. After the defeat, the confederacy at Prophet's Town dissolved. This was the beginning of the end of Tecumseh's Confederacy. The Battle of Tippecanoe would be popularized in Harrison's successful campaign for the presidency with the song-turned-slogan "Tippecanoe and Tyler Too!"

Gen'l. Harrison & Tecumseh lithograph, 1860 – Library of Congress

William Henry Harrison was well aware of Tecumseh's power. In a letter to the War Department, Harrison wrote:

"The implicit obedience and respect which the followers of Tecumseh pay to him, is really astonishing, and more than any other circumstance bespeaks him one of those

uncommon geniuses which spring up occasionally to produce revolutions and overturn the established order of things."

The Death of Tecumseh

To gain more power for his cause, Tecumseh and his allies sided with the British in the War of 1812. Fighting alongside the British in the Battle of the Thames in Ontario, Canada, Tecumseh was shot and killed in October 1813. His body was mutilated, and he was buried in a mass grave near the battlefield.

After the death of Tecumseh, the Indian Confederacy disintegrated. In addition, the end of the War of 1812 did nothing to stop the flood of American settlers moving into the Ohio River Valley. Ultimately, Tecumseh's dream of an Indian Confederacy was short-lived, but his leadership and words affected many generations.

The Death of Tecumseh, painting in the U.S. Capitol Rotunda, 1878 – Architect of the Capitol

Tecumseh's Words

"Will we let ourselves be destroyed in our turn without a struggle, to give up our homes, our country bequeathed to us by the Great Spirit, the graves of our dead and everything dear and sacred to us? I know you will cry with me, 'Never! Never!'"

A Curse?

Years after his encounters with Tecumseh, William Henry Harrison was elected president on the Whig ticket. During his 105-minute Inaugural Address on a cold, blustery March day in 1841, "Old Tippecanoe" refused to wear a coat or gloves. He fell ill shortly after the speech and died on April 4, 1841 – most likely from pneumonia. Was Harrison's death the first casualty of Tecumseh's Curse?

Including Harrison, every president elected in a year ending in zero died in office after 1840: Harrison (1840), Lincoln (1860), Garfield (1880), McKinley (1900), Harding (1920), Franklin

Roosevelt (1940), Kennedy (1960). Ronald Reagan escaped the Curse in 1981 when he was shot by John Hinckley Jr. The assassin's bullet lodged in Reagan's chest, missing his heart by inches.

The only presidential death that discredits the twenty-year cycle of the Curse was Zachary Taylor who died in 1850 after consuming bad water, milk, or cherries (His exact cause of death is unclear).

What about the presidents elected after 1840 who survived assassination attempts and were not elected on zero-years? This list includes: Theodore Roosevelt, Harry S Truman, and Gerald Ford.

So is there really a curse? There will never be evidence to confirm or deny a supposition such as Tecumseh's Curse. Nonetheless, the legend lives on. Although it is a long string of unfortunate events for seven unlucky presidents, Tecumseh's Curse remains a captivating story full of historical intrigue.

Abraham Lincoln Assassination Conspiracies

Assassination Facts

Photograph of Abraham Lincoln at Antietam.

Library of Congress
Abraham Lincoln (1809-1865) is one of the most famous Presidents of the United States. Volumes

are devoted to his life and death. However, historians have yet to unravel the mysteries surrounding his assassination. Here are the known facts:

- Abraham Lincoln and his wife, Mary Todd Lincoln attended the play, Our American Cousin at Ford's Theatre on April 14, 1865. They were to be accompanied by General Ulysses S. Grant and his wife Julia Dent Grant. However, Grant and his wife changed their plans and did not attend the play. The Lincoln's attended the play with Clara Harris and Henry Rathbone.
- During the play, actor John Wilkes Booth entered Lincoln's State Box undetected and shot him in the back of the head. He also stabbed Henry Rathbone in the arm.
- After shooting the President, Booth jumped out of the box onto the stage, broke his left leg and yelled something that some eyewitnesses reported as, "Sic Semper Tyrannus" (As always to tyrants).
- Co-conspirator Lewis Powell (or Paine/Payne) attempted to assassinate Secretary of State William Seward, but only managed to injure him. David Herold accompanied Powell. However, Herold fled before the deed was finished. At the same time, George Atzerodt was supposed to have killed Vice-President Andrew Johnson.

Atzerodt did not go through with the assassination.
- Booth and Herold escaped the Capital and traveled to Mary Surratt's Tavern in Maryland where they picked up supplies. They then traveled to Dr. Samuel Mudd's house where Booth's leg was set.
- Lincoln was taken to the Petersen House across the street from Ford's Theater where he eventually died at 7:22 A.M. April 15, 1865.
- Secretary of War Edwin Stanton stayed with the Lincolns at the Petersen House and coordinated the efforts to capture the conspirators.
- On April 26, Herold and Booth were found hiding in a barn near Port Royal, Virginia. Herold surrendered but Booth refused to come out of the barn so it was set on fire. In the ensuing chaos, a soldier shot and killed Booth.
- Eight Lincoln conspirators were caught over the next few days and tried by a military court. They were found guilty on June 30 and given various sentences depending upon their involvement. Lewis Powell (Paine), David Herold, George Atzerodt and Mary Surratt were charged with conspiring with Booth along with various other crimes and hanged on July 7, 1865. Dr. Samuel Mudd was charged with conspiring with Booth and

sentenced to life in prison. Andrew Johnson eventually pardoned him early in 1869. Samuel Arnold and Michael O'Laughlen had conspired with Booth to kidnap President Lincoln and were found guilty and sentenced to life. O'Laughlen died in prison but Arnold was pardoned by Johnson in 1869. Edman Spangler was found guilty of helping Booth escape from Ford's Theater. He was also pardoned by Johnson in 1869.

As stated before, these are the known facts. However, who was really involved in the death of Abraham Lincoln? Over the years, numerous theories have arisen to try and shed light on how this terrible tragedy could have occurred. On the following pages, a few of these theories will be explained in depth.

Pre-Assassination: Abduction

Was assassination the first goal? The general consensus today is that the first goal of the conspirators had been to kidnap the President. A few attempts to kidnap Lincoln fell through, and then the Confederacy surrendered to the North. Booth's thoughts turned to killing the President. Up until recent times, however, there was a great deal of speculation as to the existence of an abduction plot. Some people felt it might be used to exonerate the hanged conspirators. Even the judge advocates feared talk of an abduction plot might lead to an innocent verdict for some if not all of the conspirators. They are believed to have suppressed important evidence such as John Wilkes Booth's diary. (Hanchett, The Lincoln Murder Conspiracies, 107) On the other side, some people argued for the existence of a kidnapping plot because it bolstered their desire to connect Booth with a larger conspiracy masterminded by the Confederacy. With the abduction plot established, the question remains: Who was actually behind and involved in the assassination of the President?

The Simple Conspiracy Theory

The simple conspiracy in its most basic form states that Booth and a small group of friends at first planned to kidnap the president. This eventually resulted in assassination. In fact, the conspirators were to also assassinate Vice-President Johnson and Secretary of State Seward at the same time dealing a major blow to the government of the United States. Their goal was to give the South a chance to rise again. Booth saw himself as a hero. In his diary, John Wilkes Booth claimed that Abraham Lincoln was a tyrant and that Booth should be praised just as Brutus was for killing Julius Caesar. (Hanchett, 246) When Abraham Lincoln Secretaries Nicolay and Hay wrote their ten-volume biography of Lincoln in 1890 they "presented the assassination as a simple conspiracy." (Hanchett, 102)

The Grand Conspiracy Theory

Even though personal Secretaries of Lincoln presented the simple conspiracy as the most likely scenario, they acknowledged that Booth and his co-conspirators had 'suspicious contacts' with Confederate leaders. (Hanchett, 102). The Grand Conspiracy theory focuses on these connections between Booth and Confederate leaders in the south. Many variations exist of this theory. For example, it has been said that Booth had contact with Confederate leaders in Canada. It is worth noting that in April 1865 President Andrew Johnson issued a proclamation offering a reward for the arrest of Jefferson Davis in connection with the Lincoln assassination.

He was arrested because of the evidence by an individual named Conover who was later found to have given false testimony. The Republican Party also allowed the idea of the Grand Conspiracy to fall by the wayside because Lincoln had to be a martyr, and they did not want his reputation sullied with the idea that anyone would want him killed but a madman.

Eisenschmil's Grand Conspiracy Theory

This conspiracy theory was a fresh look at the Lincoln assassination as investigated by Otto Eisenschiml and reported in his book Why Was Lincoln Murdered? It implicated the divisive figure Secretary of War Edwin Stanton. Eisenschiml purported that the traditional explanation of Lincoln's assassination was unsatisfactory. (Hanchett, 157). This shaky theory is based on the supposition that General Grant would not have changed his plans to accompany the President to the theater on April 14th without an order. Eisenschiml reasoned that Stanton must have been involved in Grant's decision because he is the only person other than Lincoln from whom Grant would have taken orders. Eisenschiml goes on to offer ulterior motives for many of the actions Stanton took immediately after the assassination. He supposedly left one escape route out of Washington, the one Booth just happened to take. The presidential guard, John F. Parker, was never punished for leaving his post. Eisenschiml also states that the conspirators were hooded, killed and/or shipped off to a remote prison so they could never implicate anyone else. However, this is exactly the point where Eisenschiml's theory collapses as do most other grand conspiracy theories. Several of the conspirators had ample time and opportunity to speak and implicate Stanton and numerous others if a grand conspiracy truly existed. (Hanchett, 180) They were questioned many times during captivity and in fact were not hooded through the entire trial. In addition, after being pardoned and released from prison, Spangler, Mudd and Arnold never implicated anyone. One would think that men reported to hate the Union would relish the thought of toppling the leadership of the United States by implicating Stanton, one of the men instrumental in the South's destruction.

Lesser Conspiracies

Numerous other Lincoln assassination conspiracy theories exist. Two of the most interesting, albeit incredible, involve Andrew Johnson and the papacy. Members of Congress tried to implicate Andrew Johnson in the assassination. They even called a special committee to investigate in 1867. The committee could not find any links between Johnson and the killing. It is interesting to note that Congress impeached Johnson that same year.

The second theory as proposed by Emmett McLoughlin and others is that the Roman Catholic Church had reason to hate Abraham Lincoln. This is based on Lincoln's legal defense of a former Priest against the Bishop of Chicago. This theory is further enhanced by the fact that the Catholic

John H. Surratt, the son of Mary Surratt, fled America and ended up in the Vatican. However, the evidence connecting Pope Pius IX with the assassination is dubious at best.

Conclusion

The assassination of Abraham Lincoln has gone through many revisions during the past 136 years. Immediately following the tragedy, the Grand Conspiracy involving the Confederate leaders was the most widely accepted. Around the turn of the century, the Simple Conspiracy theory had gained a position of prominence. In the 1930's, Eisenschiml's Grand Conspiracy theory arose with the publication of Why Was Lincoln Murdered? In addition, the years have been sprinkled with other outlandish conspiracies to explain the assassination. As time has passed, one thing is true, Lincoln has become and will remain an American icon lauded with an impressive strength of will and given credit for saving our nation from division and moral oblivion.

Assassination of James A. Garfield

James A. Garfield assassination

President Garfield with James G. Blaine after being shot by Charles J. Guiteau

Location	Baltimore and Potomac Railroad Station, Washington, D.C.
Coordinates	38°53′31″N 77°01′13″WCoordinates: 38°53′31″N 77°01′13″W
Date	July 2, 1881 9:30 am (Eastern Time)

Target James A. Garfield
Attack type Assassination
Weapon(s) Bulldog Revolver
Deaths 1 (Garfield)
Injured (non-fatal) None

Perpetrators Charles J. Guiteau

The **assassination of President James A. Garfield** took place in Washington, D.C. on July 2, 1881, at the Baltimore and Potomac Railroad Station. Garfield was shot by Charles J. Guiteau at 9:30 am, less than four months into Garfield's term as the 20th President of the United States. Garfield died eleven weeks later on September 19, 1881, the second of four Presidents to be assassinated, following Abraham Lincoln and preceding William McKinley and John F. Kennedy. His Vice President, Chester A. Arthur, succeeded Garfield as President. Garfield also lived the longest after the shooting, compared to other presidents. Lincoln and Kennedy died less than a day after being shot and McKinley died a week later.

Background

Charles J. Guiteau

Charles Guiteau turned to politics after failing in several ventures, including theology, a law practice, bill collecting, and time in the utopian Oneida Community. He wrote a speech in support of Ulysses S. Grant called "Grant vs. Hancock", which he later revised to "Garfield vs. Hancock" after Garfield won the Republican nomination in the election of 1880. Guiteau never delivered the speech in a public setting, instead printing several hundred copies, but he believed that this speech along with his other efforts were largely responsible for Garfield's narrow victory over Winfield S. Hancock in the election of 1880. Guiteau believed he should have been awarded a diplomatic post for his vital assistance, first asking for Vienna, then settling for Paris. He loitered around Republican headquarters in New York City during the 1880 campaign, expecting rewards for his effort, to no avail. Still believing he would be rewarded; Guiteau arrived in Washington on March 5, 1881, the day after Garfield's inauguration, and obtained entrance to the White House and saw the President on March 8, 1881, dropping off a copy of his speech. He spent the next two months roaming around Washington, shuffling back and forth between the State Department and the White House, approaching various Cabinet members and other prominent Republicans and seeking support, to no avail. Guiteau was destitute and increasingly slovenly due to wearing the same clothes every day, the only clothes he owned, but he did not give up. On May 13, 1881, he was banned from the White House waiting room. On May 14, 1881, Secretary of State James G. Blaine told him never to return: "Never speak to me again of the Paris consulship as long as you live."

Contemporary illustration of Guiteau's pistol.

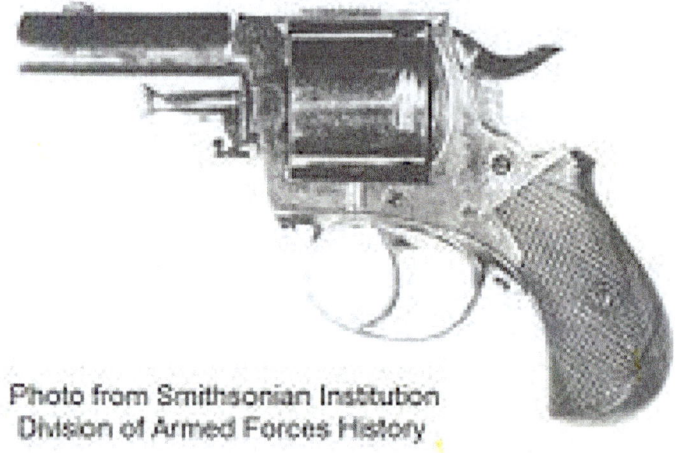

Smithsonian file photograph of the British Bulldog revolver used by Charles Guiteau to assassinate President James Garfield in 1881

Guiteau's family had judged him to be insane in 1875 and attempted to have him committed, but Guiteau had escaped. Now his mania took a violent turn. After the encounter with Blaine, Guiteau decided that he had been commanded by God to kill the ungrateful President and is quoted in saying, "I leave my justification to God." Guiteau borrowed $15 and went to purchase a revolver. He knew little about firearms, but knew that he would need a large caliber gun. He chose to buy an ivory-handled .44 Webley British Bulldog revolver over a similar wooden-handled Webley because he thought it would look good as a museum exhibit after the assassination. (The revolver was recovered and displayed by the Smithsonian in the early 20th century, but has since been lost.) He spent the next few weeks in target practice—the kick from the revolver almost knocked him over the first time—and stalking the President. He wrote a letter to Garfield, saying that he should fire Blaine, or "you and the Republican party will come to grief." The letter was ignored, as was all the correspondence Guiteau sent to the White House.

Guiteau continued to prepare carefully, writing a letter in advance to Commanding General of the United States Army William Tecumseh Sherman asking for protection from the mob, and writing other letters justifying his action as necessary to heal dissension between factions of the Republican

Party. He went to the District of Columbia jail, asking for a tour of the facility to see where he'd be incarcerated. (He was told to come back later.) Guiteau spent the whole month of June following Garfield around Washington. On one occasion, he trailed Garfield to the railway station as the President was seeing his wife off to a beach resort in Long Branch, New Jersey, but he decided to shoot him later, as Mrs. Garfield was in poor health and he did not want to upset her.

Assassination

President Garfield

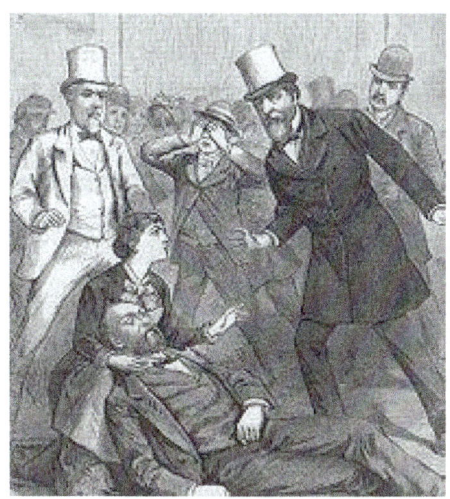

Contemporary depiction of the Garfield assassination. Secretary of State James G. Blaine stands at right.

Baltimore & Potomac Railroad Passenger Terminal, Washington, DC where U.S. President James A. Garfield was assassinated on July 2, 1881.

Garfield was scheduled to leave Washington on July 2, 1881 for his summer vacation. On that day, Guiteau lay in wait for the President at the Baltimore and Potomac Railroad station, on the southwest corner of present day Sixth Street and Constitution Avenue NW, Washington, D.C.

President Garfield came to the Sixth Street Station on his way to his alma mater, Williams College, where he was scheduled to deliver a speech. Garfield was accompanied by two of his sons, James and Harry, and Secretary of State Blaine. Secretary of War Robert Todd Lincoln waited at the station to see the President off. Garfield had no bodyguard or security detail; with the exception of Abraham Lincoln during the Civil War, early U.S. presidents never used any guards.

As President Garfield entered the waiting room of the station Guiteau stepped forward and pulled the trigger from behind at point-blank range. "My God, what is that?" Garfield cried out, flinging up his arms. Guiteau fired again and Garfield collapsed. One bullet grazed Garfield's shoulder; the other hit him in the back, passing the first lumbar vertebra but missing the spinal cord before coming to rest behind his pancreas.

Guiteau put his pistol back in his pocket and turned to leave the station for the cab he had waiting outside, but he was apprehended before he could leave by policeman Patrick Kearney, who was so excited at having arrested the man who shot the president that he neglected to take Guiteau's gun from him until after their arrival at the police station. The rapidly gathering crowd screamed "Lynch him!" but Kearney and several other police officers took Guiteau to the police station a few blocks away. As he surrendered to authorities, Guiteau uttered the exulting words, repeated everywhere: "'I am a Stalwart of the Stalwarts! I did it and I want to be arrested! Arthur is President now!'" This statement briefly led to unfounded suspicions that Arthur or his supporters had put Guiteau up to the crime. The Stalwarts were a Republican faction loyal to ex-President Grant; they strongly opposed Garfield's Half-Breeds. Like many Vice Presidents, Arthur was chosen for political advantage, to placate his faction, rather than for skills or loyalty to his running-mate. Guiteau, in his delusion, had convinced himself that he was striking a blow to unite the two factions of the Republican Party.

Garfield's suffering and death

Notice for a prayer meeting

Garfield, conscious but in shock, was carried to an upstairs floor of the train station. One bullet remained lodged in his body, but doctors could not find it. His son James Rudolph Garfield, and James Blaine, both broke down and wept. Robert Todd Lincoln, deeply upset and thinking back to the death of his father, said, "How many hours of sorrow I have passed in this town."

Garfield was carried back to the White House. Although doctors told him that he would not survive the night, the President remained conscious and alert. The next morning his vital signs were good and doctors began to hope for recovery. A long vigil began, with Garfield's doctors issuing regular bulletins that the American public followed closely throughout the summer of 1881. His condition fluctuated. Fevers came and went. Garfield struggled to keep down solid food and spent most of the summer eating little, and then only liquids.

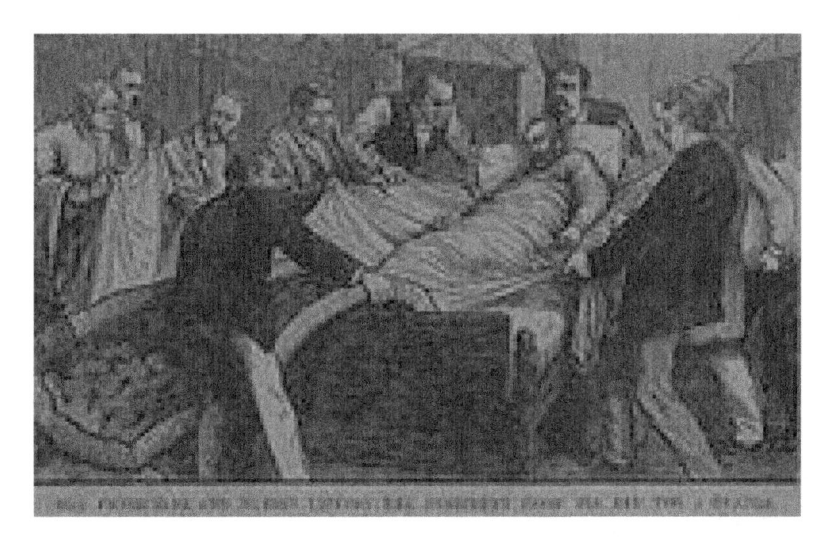

Changing Garfield's bedclothes.

In an effort to relieve the sick man from the heat of a Washington summer, Navy engineers rigged up an early version of the modern air conditioner.

Fans blew air over a large box of ice and into the President's sickroom; the device worked well enough to lower the temperature twenty degrees. Doctors continued to probe Garfield's wound with dirty, unsterilized fingers and instruments, attempting to find the location of the bullet. Alexander Graham Bell devised a metal detector specifically for the purpose of finding the bullet lodged inside Garfield, but the metal bed frame on which Garfield lay made the instrument malfunction.

On July 29, Garfield met with his Cabinet for the only time during his illness; the members were under strict instruction from the doctors not to discuss anything upsetting. Garfield became increasingly ill over a period of several weeks due to infection, which caused his heart to weaken. He remained bedridden in the White House with fevers and extreme pains. Garfield's weight dropped from over two hundred pounds to 135 pounds as his inability to keep down and digest food took its toll. Because of his inability to digest food, nutrient enemas were given in an attempt to extend his life. Blood poisoning and infection set in and for a brief period the President suffered from hallucinations. Pus-filled abscesses spread all over Garfield's body as the infections raged.

Doctors discuss Garfield's wounds.

On September 6, Garfield was taken to the Jersey Shore to escape the Washington heat, in the vain hope that the fresh air and quiet there might aid his recovery. Garfield was propped up in bed before a window with a view of the beach and ocean. New infections set in, as well as spasms of angina. He died of a ruptured splenic artery aneurysm, following blood poisoning and bronchial pneumonia, at 10:35 pm on Monday, September 19, 1881, in Elberon, New Jersey. The wounded president died exactly two months before his 50th birthday and remains one of the only two Presidents who died before their 50th birthday, the other being John F. Kennedy, who was also assassinated when he was just 46 years and 177 days old. During the eighty days between his shooting and death, his only official act was to sign an extradition paper.

The funeral in Lake View Cemetery.

Most historians and medical experts now believe that Garfield probably would have survived his wound had the doctors attending him been more capable. Unfortunately for Garfield, most American doctors of the day did not believe in anti-sepsis measures or the need for cleanliness to prevent infection. Several inserted their unsterilized fingers into the wound to probe for the bullet, and one doctor punctured Garfield's liver in doing so. Also, self-appointed chief physician D. Willard Bliss had supplanted Garfield's usual physician, Jedediah Hyde Baxter. Bliss and the other doctors who attended Garfield had guessed wrong about the path of the bullet in Garfield's body. They had erroneously probed rightward into Garfield's back instead of leftward, missing the location of the bullet but creating a new channel which filled with pus. The autopsy not only discovered this error but revealed pneumonia in both lungs and a body that was filled with pus due to uncontrolled septicemia.

Chester Arthur was at his home in New York City when word came the night of September 19 that Garfield had died. After first getting the news, Arthur said "I hope—my God, I do hope it is a mistake." But confirmation by telegram came soon after. Arthur took the presidential oath of office, administered by a New York Supreme Court judge, then left for Long Branch to pay his respects before going on to Washington.

Garfield's body was taken to Washington, where it lay in state for two days in the Capitol Rotunda before being taken to Cleveland, where the funeral was held on September 26.

Guiteau's trial and execution

President Garfield's casket lying in state at the Capitol Rotunda.

Guiteau went on trial in November. Represented by his brother-in-law, George Scolville, Guiteau became something of a media darling during his trial for his bizarre behavior, including constantly insulting his defense team, formatting his testimony in epic poems which he recited at length, and soliciting legal advice from random spectators in the audience via passed notes. He claimed that he was not guilty because Garfield's murder was the will of God and he was only an instrument of God's will. He sang "John Brown's Body" to the court. He dictated an autobiography to the *New York Herald*, ending it with a personal ad for a nice Christian lady under thirty. He was blissfully oblivious to the American public's outrage and hatred of him, even after he was almost assassinated twice himself. At one point, he argued that Garfield was killed not by him but by medical malpractice ("I deny the killing, if your honor please. We admit the shooting"), which was essentially true, if one discounts the fact that Guiteau was the reason the President required medical attention in the first place. Throughout the trial and up until his execution, Guiteau was housed at St. Elizabeths Hospital in the southeastern quadrant of Washington, D.C.

Guiteau's trial was one of the first high profile cases in the United States where the insanity defense was considered. Guiteau vehemently insisted that while he had been legally insane at the time of the shooting, he was not really medically insane, which was one of the major causes of the rift between him and his defense lawyers and probably also a reason the jury assumed Guiteau was merely trying to deny responsibility.

To the end, Guiteau was actively making plans to start a lecture tour after his perceived imminent release and to run for President himself in 1884, while at the same time continuing to delight in the media circus surrounding his trial. He was dismayed when the jury was unconvinced of his divine inspiration, convicting him of the murder.

He was found guilty on January 25, 1882. He appealed, but his appeal was rejected, and he was hanged on June 30, 1882 in the District of Columbia. At his execution, Guiteau famously danced his way up to the gallows and while on the scaffold he waved at the audience, shook hands with his executioner and, as a last request, recited a poem he had written called "I am Going to the Lordy". He had requested an orchestra to play as he sang his poem, but this request was denied.

Aftermath

The Garfield Monument at the U.S. Capitol

Part of Charles Guiteau's preserved brain is on display at the Mütter Museum at the College of Physicians of Philadelphia. Guiteau's bones and more of his brain, along with Garfield's backbone and a couple of ribs, are kept at the National Museum of Health and Medicine in Washington, D.C. on the grounds of the Walter Reed Army Medical Center.

Mourners pass Garfield's body. Front L–R, Secretary of State James G. Blaine, President Chester A. Arthur and former President Ulysses S. Grant

Garfield's assassination was instrumental to the passage of the Pendleton Civil Service Reform Act on January 16, 1883. Garfield himself had called for civil service reform in his inaugural address and supported it as President in the belief that it would make government more efficient. It was passed as something of a memorial to the fallen President. Arthur lost the Republican Party nomination in 1884 to Blaine, who went on to lose a close election to Democrat Grover Cleveland.

The Sixth Street rail station was later demolished. The site is now occupied by the West Building of the National Gallery of Art. No plaque or memorial marks the spot where Garfield was shot, but a few blocks away, a Garfield memorial statue stands on the southwest corner of the Capitol grounds.

The question of Presidential disability was not addressed. Article II, section 1, clause 6 of the Constitution says that in case of the "Inability [of the President] to discharge the Powers and Duties of the said Office, the same shall devolve on the Vice President", but gives no further instruction on what constitutes inability or how the President's inability should be determined. Garfield had lain on his sickbed for 80 days without performing any of the duties of his office except for the signing of an extradition paper, but this did not prove to be a difficulty because in the 19th century the federal government effectively shut down for the summer regardless. During Garfield's ordeal, the Congress was not in session and there was little for a President to do. Blaine suggested the Cabinet declare Arthur acting President, but this option was rejected by all, including Arthur, who did not wish to be perceived as grasping for power.

The Garfield Tea House in October 2007.

Congress did not deal with the problem of what to do if a President was alive but incapacitated as Garfield was. Nor did the Congress take up the question 38 years later, when Woodrow Wilson suffered a stroke that put him in a coma for days and left him partially paralyzed and blind in one eye for the last year and a half of his Presidency. It was not until the ratification of the Twenty-fifth Amendment to the United States Constitution in 1967 that United States law provided a procedure for what to do if the President were incapacitated.

Only sixteen years had passed between the first and second Presidential assassinations. Nevertheless, whereas Lincoln's assassination had taken place in the closing stages of the Civil War, both the public and the country's political leaders were keen to consider Garfield's murder to be an isolated act unlikely to be repeated in peacetime. Perhaps because the outrage as expressed in newspaper editorials focused specifically on the failure to adequately deal with the rejected office-seeker Guiteau as opposed to the inadequate security protecting the President, the Congress failed to take any measure to provide for Presidential protection. It was not until after the assassination of William McKinley twenty years after Garfield's assassination, that the Congress charged the United States Secret Service, originally founded to prevent counterfeiting, with Presidential security.

The Garfield Tea House, built by the citizens of Long Branch, New Jersey with the railroad ties that had been laid down specifically to give Garfield's train access to their town, still stands today near the location where Garfield died.

U.S. President William McKinley Assassinated (1901):
On September 6, 1901, U.S. President William McKinley spent the morning visiting Niagara Falls with his wife before returning to the Pan-American Exposition in Buffalo, New York in the afternoon to spend a few minutes greeting the public.

By about 3:30 p.m., President McKinley stood inside the Temple of Music building at the Exposition, ready to begin shaking the hands of the public as they streamed into the building. Many had been waiting for hours outside in the heat for their chance to meet the President. Unbeknownst to the President and the many guards who stood nearby, among those waiting outside was 28-year-old anarchist Leon Czolgosz who was planning to kill President McKinley.

At 4 p.m. the doors to the building were opened and the mass of people waiting outside were forced into a single line as they entered the Temple of Music building. The line of people thus came up to the president in an organized fashion, with just enough time to whisper a "Nice to meet you, Mr. President," shake President McKinley's hand, and then be forced to continue along the line and out the door again.

President McKinley, the 25th president of the United States, was a popular president who had just started his second term in office and the people seemed clearly glad to get a chance to meet him. However, at 4:07 p.m. Leon Czolgosz had made it into the building and it was his turn to greet the President.

In Czolgosz's right hand, he held a .32 caliber Iver-Johnson revolver, which he had covered by wrapping a handkerchief around the gun and his hand. Although Czolgosz's swaddled hand was noticed before he reached the President, many thought it looked like it covered an injury and not that it was hiding a gun. Also, since the day had been hot, many of the visitors to see the President had been carrying handkerchiefs in their hands so that they could wipe the sweat off their faces.

When Czolgosz reached the President, President McKinley reached out to shake his left hand (thinking Czolgosz's right hand was injured) while Czolgosz brought up his right hand to President McKinley's chest and then fired two shots.

One of the bullets didn't enter the president - some say it bounced off of a button or off the president's sternum and then got tucked into his clothing. The other bullet, however, entered the president's abdomen, tearing through his stomach, pancreas, and kidney. Shocked at being shot, President McKinley began to sag as blood stained his white shirt. He then told those around him, "Be careful how you tell my wife."

Those in line behind Czolgosz and guards in the room all jumped on Czolgosz and started to punch him. Seeing that the mob on Czolgosz might easily and quickly kill him, President McKinley whispered either, "Don't let them hurt him" or "Go easy on him, boys."

President McKinley was then whisked away in an electric ambulance to the hospital at the Exposition. Unfortunately, the hospital was not properly equipped for such a surgery and the very experienced doctor usually on premises was away doing a surgery in another town. Although several doctors were found, the most experienced doctor that could be found was Dr. Matthew Mann, a gynecologist. The surgery began at 5:20 p.m.

During the operation, the doctors searched for the remains of the bullet that had entered the President's abdomen, but were unable to locate it. Worried that continued searching would tax the President's body too much, the doctors decided to discontinue looking for it and to sew up what they could. The surgery was completed a little before 7 p.m.

For several days, President McKinley seemed to be getting better. After the shock of the shooting, the nation was excited to hear some good news. However, what the doctors did not realize was that without drainage, an infection had built up inside the President. By September 13 it was obvious the President was dying. At 2:15 a.m. on September 14, 1901, President William McKinley died of gangrene. That afternoon, Vice President Theodore Roosevelt was sworn in as President of the United States.

After being pummeled right after the shooting, Leon Czolgosz had been arrested and taken to police headquarters before nearly being lynched by the angry crowds that surrounded the Temple of Music. Czolgosz readily admitted that he was the one who had shot the President. In his written confession, Czolgosz stated, "I killed President McKinley because I done my duty. I didn't believe one man should have so much service and another man should have none."

Czolgosz was brought to trial on September 23, 1901. He was quickly found guilty and sentenced to death. On October 29, 1901, Leon Czolgosz was electrocuted.

November 22, 1963: Death of the President

Shortly after noon on November 22, 1963, President John F. Kennedy was assassinated as he rode in a motorcade through Dealey Plaza in downtown Dallas, Texas.

By the fall of 1963, President John F. Kennedy and his political advisers were preparing for the next presidential campaign. Although he had not formally announced his candidacy, it was clear that President Kennedy was going to run and he seemed confident about his chances for re-election.

At the end of September, the president traveled west, speaking in nine different states in less than a week. The trip was meant to put a spotlight on natural resources and conservation efforts. But JFK also used it to sound out themes—such as education, national security, and world peace—for his run in 1964.

Campaigning in Texas

A month later, the president addressed Democratic gatherings in Boston and Philadelphia. Then, on November 12, he held the first important political planning session for the upcoming election year. At the meeting, JFK stressed the importance of winning Florida and Texas and talked about his plans to visit both states in the next two weeks. Mrs. Kennedy would accompany him on the swing through Texas, which would be her first extended public appearance since the loss of their baby, Patrick, in August. On November 21, the president and first lady departed on Air Force One for the two-day, five-city tour of Texas.

President Kennedy was aware that a feud among party leaders in Texas could jeopardize his chances of carrying the state in 1964, and one of his aims for the trip was to bring Democrats together. He also knew that a relatively small but vocal group of extremists was contributing to the political tensions in Texas and would likely make its presence felt—particularly in Dallas, where U.S. Ambassador to the United Nations Adlai Stevenson had been physically attacked a month earlier after making a speech there. Nonetheless, JFK seemed to relish the prospect of leaving Washington, getting out among the people and into the political fray.

The first stop was San Antonio. Vice President Lyndon B. Johnson, Governor John B. Connally, and Senator Ralph W. Yarborough led the welcoming party. They accompanied the president to Brooks Air Force Base for the dedication of the Aerospace Medical Health Center. Continuing on to Houston, he addressed a Latin American citizens' organization and spoke at a testimonial dinner for Congressman Albert Thomas before ending the day in Fort Worth.

Morning in Fort Worth

A light rain was falling on Friday morning, November 22, but a crowd of several thousand stood in the parking lot outside the Texas Hotel where the Kennedys had spent the night. A platform was set up and the president, wearing no protection against the weather, came out to make some brief remarks. "There are no faint hearts in Fort Worth," he began, "and I appreciate your being here this morning. Mrs. Kennedy is organizing herself. It takes longer, but, of course, she looks better than we do when she does it." He went on to talk about the nation's need for being "second to none" in defense and in space, for continued growth in the economy and "the willingness of citizens of the United States to assume the burdens of leadership."

The warmth of the audience response was palpable as the president reached out to shake hands amidst a sea of smiling faces.

Back inside the hotel the president spoke at a breakfast of the Fort Worth Chamber of Commerce, focusing on military preparedness. "We are still the keystone in the arch of freedom," he said. "We will continue to do…our duty, and the people of Texas will be in the lead."

On to Dallas

The presidential party left the hotel and went by motorcade to Carswell Air Force Base for the thirteen-minute flight to Dallas. Arriving at Love Field, President and Mrs. Kennedy disembarked and immediately walked toward a fence where a crowd of well-wishers had gathered, and they spent several minutes shaking hands.

The first lady received a bouquet of red roses, which she brought with her to the waiting limousine. Governor John Connally and his wife, Nellie, were already seated in the open convertible as the Kennedys entered and sat behind them. Since it was no longer raining, the plastic bubble top had been left off. Vice President and Mrs. Johnson occupied another car in the motorcade.

The procession left the airport and traveled along a ten-mile route that wound through downtown Dallas on the way to the Trade Mart where the President was scheduled to speak at a luncheon.

The Assassination

Crowds of excited people lined the streets and waved to the Kennedys. The car turned off Main Street at Dealey Plaza around 12:30 p.m. As it was passing the Texas School Book Depository, gunfire suddenly reverberated in the plaza.

Bullets struck the president's neck and head and he slumped over toward Mrs. Kennedy. The governor was also hit in the chest.

The car sped off to Parkland Memorial Hospital just a few minutes away. But little could be done for the President.

A Catholic priest was summoned to administer the last rites, and at 1:00 p.m. John F. Kennedy was pronounced dead. Though seriously wounded, Governor Connally would recover.

The president's body was brought to Love Field and placed on *Air Force One*. Before the plane took off, a grim-faced Lyndon B. Johnson stood in the tight, crowded compartment and took the oath of office, administered by U.S. District Court Judge Sarah Hughes. The brief ceremony took place at 2:38 p.m.

Less than an hour earlier, police had arrested Lee Harvey Oswald, a recently hired employee at the Texas School Book Depository. He was being held for the assassination of President Kennedy and the fatal shooting, shortly afterward, of Patrolman J. D. Tippit on a Dallas street.

On Sunday morning, November 24, Oswald was scheduled to be transferred from police headquarters to the county jail. Viewers across America watching the live television coverage suddenly saw a man aim a pistol and fire at point blank range. The assailant was identified as Jack Ruby, a local nightclub owner. Oswald died two hours later at Parkland Hospital.

The President's Funeral

That same day, President Kennedy's flag-draped casket was moved from the White House to the Capitol on a caisson drawn by six grey horses, accompanied by one rider-less black horse. At Mrs. Kennedy's request, the cortege and other ceremonial details were modeled on the funeral of Abraham Lincoln. Crowds lined Pennsylvania Avenue and many wept openly as the caisson passed. During the 21 hours that the president's body lay in state in the Capitol Rotunda, about 250,000 people filed by to pay their respects.

On Monday, November 25, 1963 President Kennedy was laid to rest in Arlington National Cemetery. The funeral was attended by heads of state and representatives from more than 100 countries, with untold millions more watching on television. Afterward, at the grave site, Mrs. Kennedy and her husband's brothers, Robert and Edward, lit an eternal flame.

Perhaps the most indelible images of the day were the salute to his father given by little John F. Kennedy, Jr. (whose third birthday it was), daughter Caroline kneeling next to her mother at the president's bier, and the extraordinary grace and dignity shown by Jacqueline Kennedy.

As people throughout the nation and the world struggled to make sense of a senseless act and to articulate their feelings about President Kennedy's life and legacy, many recalled these words from his inaugural address:

All this will not be finished in the first one hundred days, nor in the first one thousand days, nor in the life of this administration. Nor even perhaps in our lifetime on this planet. But let us begin.

The Warren Commission

On November 29, 1963 President Lyndon B. Johnson appointed the President's Commission on the Assassination of President Kennedy. It came to be known as the Warren Commission after its chairman, Earl Warren, Chief Justice of the United States. President Johnson directed the commission to evaluate matters relating to the assassination and the subsequent killing of the alleged assassin, and to report its findings and conclusions to him. To see the Warren Commission's report, go to http://www.archives.gov/research/jfk/warren-commission-report/index.html

The House Select Committee on Assassinations

The U.S. House of Representatives established the House Select Committee on Assassinations in 1976 to reopen the investigation of the assassination in light of allegations that previous inquiries had not received the full cooperation of federal agencies.

President Andrew Jackson Survived an Assassination Attempt

Andrew Jackson

Library of Congress

President Andrew Jackson, perhaps the most combative American president ever, not only survived an assassination attempt, he tried to assault the man who had tried to shoot him.

On January 30, 1835, Andrew Jackson visited the U.S. Capitol to attend the funeral of a member of Congress. While on his way out of the building a man named Richard Lawrence stepped out from behind a pillar and fired a flintlock pistol. The gun misfired, making a loud noise but not firing a projectile.

As shocked spectators looked on, Lawrence pulled out another pistol and again pulled the trigger. The second pistol also misfired, again making a loud, though harmless, noise.

Jackson, who had survived countless violent encounters, one of which left a pistol ball in his body that wasn't removed for decades, flew into a rage. As several people grabbed Lawrence and wrestled him to the ground, Jackson reportedly struck the failed assassin several times with his cane.

Jackson's Attacker Was Put On Trial

Richard Lawrence was rescued from the hands of a very angry President Andrew Jackson, and was immediately arrested. He was put on trial in the spring of 1835. The prosecutor for the government was Francis Scott Key, a prominent attorney remembered today for being the author of the "Star-Spangled Banner."

Newspaper reports from the trial detail that Lawrence was visited by a doctor in prison and the doctor found him to be suffering from "morbid delusions." He apparently believed that he was the king of the United States and Andrew Jackson had taken his rightful place at the nation's leader. Lawrence also contended that Jackson had plotted against him in various ways.

Lawrence was found not guilty by reason of insanity, and was kept in various mental institutions until his death in 1861.

Andrew Jackson had made many enemies in his life, and his presidency was marked with such controversies as the Nullification Crisis, the Bank War, and the Spoils System.

So there were many who believed that Lawrence might have been part of some conspiracy. But the most reasonable explanation is that Richard Lawrence was insane and acted alone.

Shot in the Chest 100 Years Ago, Teddy Roosevelt Kept on Talking

On October 14, 1912, an unemployed saloonkeeper shot former president and Progressive Party candidate Theodore Roosevelt outside a Milwaukee hotel. Rather than being rushed to the hospital, Roosevelt insisted on delivering his scheduled 90-minute speech. By slowing the bullet, those lengthy prepared remarks may actually have saved his life.

Theodore Roosevelt shortly before John Schrank made an attempt on his life. (Library of Congress)

Theodore Roosevelt's opening line was hardly remarkable for a presidential campaign speech: "Friends, I shall ask you to be as quiet as possible." His second line, however, was a bombshell.

"I don't know whether you fully understand that I have just been shot."

Clearly, Roosevelt had buried the lede. The horrified audience in the Milwaukee Auditorium on October 14, 1912, gasped as the former president unbuttoned his vest to reveal his bloodstained shirt. "It takes more than that to kill a bull moose," the wounded candidate assured them. He reached into his coat pocket and pulled out a bullet-riddled, 50-page speech. Holding up his prepared remarks, which had two big holes blown through each page, Roosevelt continued. "Fortunately I had my manuscript, so you see I was going to make a long speech, and there is a bullet—there is where the bullet went through—and it probably saved me from it going into my heart. The bullet is in me now, so that I cannot make a very long speech, but I will try my best."

Only two days before, the editor-in-chief of The Outlook characterized Roosevelt as "an electric battery of inexhaustible energy," and for the next 90 minutes the 53-year-old former president proved it. "I give you my word, I do not care a rap about being shot; not a rap," he claimed. Few could doubt him. Although his voice weakened and his breath shortened, Roosevelt glared at his nervous aides whenever they begged him to stop speaking or positioned themselves around the podium to catch him if he collapsed. Only with the speech completed did he agree to visit the hospital.

The damaged eyeglass case that helped slow the trajectory of the bullet that hit Theodore Roosevelt. (National Park Service)

The shooting had occurred just after 8 p.m. as Roosevelt entered his car outside the Gilpatrick Hotel. As he stood up in the open-air automobile and waved his hat with his right hand to the crowd, a flash from a Colt revolver 5 feet away lit up the night. The candidate's stenographer quickly put the would-be assassin in a half nelson and grabbed the assailant's right wrist to prevent him from firing a second shot.

The well-wishing crowd morphed into a bloodthirsty pack, raining blows on the shooter and shouting, "Kill him!" According to an eyewitness, one man was "the coolest and least excited of anyone in the frenzied mob": Roosevelt. The man who had been propelled to the Oval Office after an assassin felled President William McKinley bellowed out, "Don't hurt him. Bring him here. I want to see him." Roosevelt asked the shooter, "What did you do it for?" With no answer forthcoming, he said, "Oh, what's the use? Turn him over to the police."

Although there were no outward signs of blood, the former president reached inside his heavy overcoat and felt a dime-sized bullet hole on the right side of his chest. "He pinked me," Roosevelt told a party official. He coughed into his hand three times. Not seeing any telltale blood, he determined that the bullet hadn't penetrated his lungs. An accompanying doctor naturally told the driver to head directly to the hospital, but Colonel Roosevelt gave different marching orders: "You get me to that speech."

X-rays taken after the campaign event showed the bullet lodged against Roosevelt's fourth right rib on an upward path to his heart. Fortunately, the projectile had been slowed by his dense overcoat, steel-reinforced eyeglass case and hefty speech squeezed into his inner right jacket pocket. Roosevelt dictated a telegram to his wife that said he was "in excellent shape" and that the "trivial" wound wasn't "a particle more serious than one of the injuries any of the boys used continually to be having."

John Schrank after his arrest. (Library of Congress)

Even before the shooting, the 1912 presidential campaign had been a raucous one, with the former Republican president challenging his party's standard-bearer (and his handpicked successor), incumbent William Howard Taft. The internecine fight, so fierce that barbed wire concealed by patriotic bunting defended the podium at the Republican Convention, tore the Grand Old Party apart. Roosevelt went rogue and ran under the banner of the Progressive Party, nicknamed the "Bull Moose Party." Blasted by political opponents and elements of the press for being a power-hungry traitor willing to break the tradition of two-term presidencies, Roosevelt told the Milwaukee audience that the campaign's inflamed political rhetoric contributed to the shooting. "It is a very natural thing," he said, "that weak and vicious minds should be inflamed to acts of violence by the kind of awful mendacity and abuse that have been heaped upon me for the last three months by the papers."

The "weak" mind responsible for the assassination attempt belonged to 36-year-old John Schrank, an unemployed New York City saloonkeeper who had stalked his prey around the country for weeks. A handwritten screed found in his pockets reflected the troubled thoughts of a paranoid schizophrenic. "To the people of the United States," Schrank had written. "In a dream I saw President McKinley sit up in his coffin pointing at a man in a monk's attire in whom I recognized Theodore Roosevelt. The dead president said—This is my murderer—avenge my death." Schrank also claimed he acted to defend the two-term tradition of American presidents. "I did not intend to kill the citizen Roosevelt," the shooter said at his trial. "I intended to kill Theodore Roosevelt, the third termer." Schrank pled guilty, was determined to be insane and was confined for life in a Wisconsin state asylum.

Doctors determined it was safer to leave the bullet embedded deep in Roosevelt's chest than to operate, although the shooting exacerbated his chronic rheumatoid arthritis for the rest of his life. Even though the attempted assassination unleashed a wave of sympathy for Roosevelt, the Republican split led to an easy victory by Democrat Woodrow Wilson on Election Day. Roosevelt came in second with 27 percent of the vote, the highest percentage of any third-party candidate in American history.

1933 - Assassination Attempt on Franklin D. Roosevelt

Giuseppe Zangara

Giuseppe Zangara

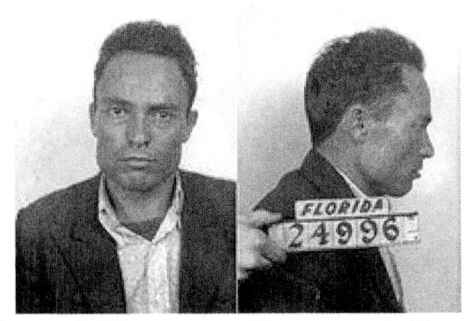

Mug shot of Giuseppe Zangara following his arrest.

Born	September 7, 1900 Ferruzzano, Calabria, Kingdom of Italy
Died	March 20, 1933 (aged 32) Florida State Prison, Raiford, Florida, U.S.
Occupation	Bricklayer
Criminal charge	First-degree murder

Criminal penalty	Death by electric chair
Criminal status	Deceased

Giuseppe Zangara (September 7, 1900 – March 20, 1933) was the assassin of Chicago mayor Anton Cermak, though United States President–elect Franklin D. Roosevelt may have been his intended target. Roosevelt escaped injury, but five people were shot including Cermak.

Early life

Zangara was born in Ferruzzano, Calabria, Italy. After serving in the Tyrolian Alps in World War I, Zangara did a variety of menial jobs in his home village before immigrating with his uncle to the United States in 1923. He settled in Paterson, New Jersey and on September 11, 1929, he became a naturalized citizen of the United States.

Physical health problems

Zangara, a poorly educated bricklayer, suffered severe pain in his abdomen, later attributed to adhesions of the gall bladder, possibly originating from an appendectomy performed in 1926. These adhesions were later cited as a cause for his increasing mental delusions. It became increasingly difficult for him to work due to both his physical and mental conditions.

Assassination attempt

On February 15, 1933, Roosevelt was giving an impromptu speech from the back of an open car in the Bayfront Park area of Miami, Florida, where Zangara was living, working the occasional odd job, and living off his savings. Zangara joined the crowd, armed with a .32-caliber pistol he had bought at a local pawn shop. However, being only five feet tall, he was unable to see over other people, and had to stand on a wobbly, metal folding chair, peering over the hat of Lillian Cross to get a clear aim at his target. After the first shot, Cross and others grabbed his arm, and he fired four more shots wildly. Five people were hit, including Chicago mayor Anton Cermak, who was standing on the running board of the car next to Roosevelt. En route to the hospital, Cermak allegedly told FDR, "I'm glad it was me instead of you", words now inscribed on a plaque in Bayfront Park.

Aftermath

In the Dade County Courthouse jail, Zangara confessed and stated: "I have the gun in my hand. I kill kings and presidents first and next all capitalists." He pleaded guilty to four counts of attempted murder and was sentenced to 80 years in prison. As he was led out of the courtroom, Zangara told the judge: "Four times 20 is 80. Oh, judge, don't be stingy. Give me a hundred years." The judge, aware that Cermak might not survive his wounds, replied: "Maybe there will be more later."

Cermak died of peritonitis 19 days later, on March 6, 1933, two days after Roosevelt's inauguration. Zangara was promptly indicted for first-degree murder in Cermak's death. Because Zangara had intended to commit murder, it was irrelevant that his intended target may not have been the man he ultimately killed. In that case, he would still be guilty of murder under the doctrine of transferred intent.

Zangara pleaded guilty to the additional murder charge, and was sentenced to death by Circuit Court Judge Uly Thompson. Zangara said after hearing his sentence: "You give me electric chair. I no afraid of that chair! You one of capitalists. You is crook man too. Put me in electric chair. I no care!" Under Florida law, a convicted murderer could not share cell space with another prisoner before his execution, but another convicted murderer was already awaiting execution at Raiford. Zangara's sentence required prison officials to expand their waiting area, and the "death cell" became "Death Row".

Execution

On March 20, 1933, after spending only 10 days on Death Row, Zangara was executed in Old Sparky, the electric chair at Florida State Prison in Raiford, Florida. Zangara became enraged when he learned no newsreel cameras would be filming his final moments. Zangara's final statement was "Viva Italia! Goodbye to all poor peoples everywhere! [...] Pusha da button!"

Motivations

Raymond Moley interviewed Zangara and believed he was not part of any larger plot, and that he had intended to kill Roosevelt.

Alternative theories have circulated, especially in Chicago, where there were rumors that Zangara was a hired killer, working for Frank Nitti, who was the head of the Chicago Outfit (Chicago's largest organized-crime syndicate). Allegedly, Mayor Cermak was the real target, because of his pledge to clean up the rampant gang violence in Chicago. Another speculation is that Cermak was connected to the Outfit's underworld rivals.

Some versions of this story assert that Zangara was a diversion for a second gunman who was to shoot Cermak; but this alleged second gunman was never seen.

Another point is that Zangara had been an expert marksman in the Italian Army (though not with a pistol from a great distance), and would presumably hit his target, so perhaps Cermak was the intended victim.

In popular culture

Zangara was played by Eddie Korbich in the original Off-Broadway production of *Assassins* by Stephen Sondheim. In later productions he was played by Paul Harrhy in London and by Jeffrey Kuhn in the show's original Broadway production. Appearing in several songs from the play, he has a major solo in the number, "How I Saved Roosevelt".

Zangara plays a significant role in the background provided for Philip K. Dick's *The Man in the High Castle*. The alternate history novel begins with the premise that Zangara succeeded in assassinating Franklin D. Roosevelt, using this historical event as its point of divergence - leading eventually to Axis victory in World War II.

In 1960, in a two-part story line titled; 'The Unhired Assassin' on the TV show *The Untouchables*, actor Joe Mantell played the part of Giuseppe "Joe" Zangara. This episode, while depicting Zangara's story throughout, focuses mostly on Nitti's plan to kill Mayor Cermak, with an initial (fictionalised) attempt in Chicago which is foiled by Ness & his agents at the end of 'part one', then in 'part two' using a contract hitman, an ex-Army rifleman in Florida which again fails, thanks to Eliot Ness (played by Robert Stack). But Ness's successful prevention of Nitti's assassination plot is quickly undercut when Zangara does the deed. The shows were originally aired February 25 and March 3, 1960.This two part story was later edited together as a feature length story retitled; 'The Gun of Zangara'

Max Allan Collins' 1983 novel, *True Detective*, first in the Nathan Heller mystery series, features Zangara's attempted assassination of Roosevelt, positing it as an actual attempt on Chicago's mayor at the time, Anton Cermak. The novel won the 1984 Shamus Award for Best P.I. Hardcover from the Private Eye Writers of America.

The 2011 fantasy noir novel *Spellbound* by Larry Correia features Zangara's attempted assassination of FDR. Zangara is magically enhanced in a plot to inflame bigotry and curtail the civil rights of the magically gifted protagonists of the Grimnoir

Society. Instead of using a small caliber handgun, Zangara is made into a living cannon or bomb, and kills nearly 200 onlookers including Mayor Cermak and crippling Roosevelt.

Truman assassination attempt

Truman assassination attempt

Harry S. Truman

Location	Blair House Washington, D.C.
Date	November 1, 1950
Target	Harry S. Truman
Weapon(s)	Walther P38, Luger pistol
Deaths	Two; Leslie Coffelt, Griselio Torresola
Injured (non-	Three; Donald Birdzell,

fatal)	Oscar Collazo, Joseph Downs
Perpetrators	Oscar Collazo, Griselio Torresola
Motive	Political status of Puerto Rico

The second of two assassination attempts on U.S. President Harry S. Truman occurred on November 1, 1950. It was carried out by two Puerto Rican pro-independence activists, Oscar Collazo and Griselio Torresola, while the President resided at the Blair House. Torresola mortally wounded White House Police officer Leslie Coffelt, who killed him in return fire. Secret Service agents also were involved and wounded Collazo. President Harry S. Truman was not harmed.

In an unrelated incident in 1947, the Secret Service had arranged to intercept and defuse some letter bombs addressed to Truman and his top staff after being alerted by British Intelligence, who had discovered similar letters sent to high-ranking British officials by the Zionist Stern Gang. This was during the period when the United Nations was reviewing the British mandate in Palestine. Truman supported recognition of an independent Israel in 1948.

1947 incident

In the summer of 1947, pending the independence of Israel, the Zionist Stern Gang was believed to have sent a number of letter bombs addressed to the president and high-ranking staff at the White House. The Secret Service had been alerted by British intelligence after similar letters had been sent to high-ranking British officials and the Gang claimed credit. The mail room of the White House intercepted the letters and the Secret Service defused them. At the time, the incident was not publicized. Truman's daughter Margaret confirmed the incident in her biography of Truman published in 1972. It had earlier been told in a memoir by Ira R.T. Smith, who worked in the mail room.

Background to 1950 Puerto Rican attempt

In the 1940s, the Nationalist Party of Puerto Rico had little political power in the country, where voters had elected the Popular Democratic Party of Puerto Rico (PPD) as the majority in the legislature. Nationalist believed that Puerto Rico still suffered from American colonialism and wanted independence. The Popular Democratic Party of Puerto Rico (PPD) was supporting negotiations with the United States to create a "new" political status for the island.

This led to the Puerto Rican Nationalist Party Revolts of the 1950s, an armed protest for independence by the Puerto Rican Nationalist Party against United States Government rule over Puerto Rico. The Party repudiated the "Free Associated State" (*Estado Libre Asociado*) status that had been enacted in 1950, as the Nationalists considered it to be a continuation of colonialism.

The revolts began on October 30, 1950, upon the orders of Pedro Albizu Campos, president of the Nationalist Party. Uprisings occurred in Peñuelas, Mayagüez, Naranjito, Arecibo and Ponce. The most notable uprisings occurred in Utuado, Jayuya, and San Juan. These were suppressed by strong military force, including the use of planes.

Plans for the assassination

Griselio Torresola

In New York City, the Nationalists Griselio Torresola and Oscar Collazo developed a plan to assassinate the U.S. President, Harry S. Truman in order to demonstrate that the October 30 uprising had not been an "incident between Puerto Ricans" as described by President Truman, but rather was a sign of a war between two countries. They had learned that Truman was living at the Blair House, while the White House was renovated.

Oscar Collazo

The two men realized that their attempt was near-suicidal, and that they likely would be killed. Nonetheless, they wanted to bring world attention to the government killings of rebels and associates in Puerto Rico, and the need for Puerto Rican independence. Torresola, a skilled gunman, taught Collazo how to load and handle a gun. They took the train to Washington, DC to reconnoiter the area. On November 1, 1950, they attacked.

Attack

Blair House, site of the attempt, as it is today. At the time, there were two guard booths in front, which are not present today.

Torresola approached along Pennsylvania Avenue from the west side, while his partner, Oscar Collazo, walked up behind Capitol police officer, Donald Birdzell, who was standing on the steps of the Blair House. While President Truman napped on the second floor, Collazo shot at Birdzell, but had failed to chamber a round in it, and the gun did not fire. After fumbling with it, Collazo fired the weapon just as Birdzell was turning to face him, and shot the officer in his right knee.

After hearing the gunshots, Secret Service agent Vincent Mroz ran through a basement corridor and stepped out of a street-level door on the east side of the House, where he opened fire on Collazo. Mroz stopped Collazo on the outside steps with a bullet to the chest. The incident has been described as "the biggest gunfight in Secret Service history." Two other officers took part in the shooting of the attackers.

Meanwhile, Torresola had approached a guard booth at the west corner and took White House police officer Leslie Coffelt by surprise, shooting at him four times from close range and mortally wounding him with a 9mm German Luger. Three of those shots struck Coffelt in the chest and abdomen, and the fourth went through his tunic.

Torresola shot police officer Joseph Downs in the hip, before he could draw his weapon. As Downs turned toward the house, Torresola shot him in the back and in the neck. Downs got into the basement and secured the door, denying Torresola entry into the Blair House.

Torresola turned his attention to the shoot-out between his partner Collazo and several other police officers. He shot Officer Donald Birdzell in the left knee.

White House Policeman Leslie W. Coffelt

Birdzell could no longer stand and was effectively incapacitated (he would later recover).

Torresola stood to the left of the Blair House steps to reload. President Truman had awakened from a nap to the sound of gunfire and looked outside his second floor window. Torresola was 31 feet (9.4 m) away from Truman's window. Secret Service agents shouted at Truman to get away from the window.

At that same moment, Coffelt left the guard booth, propped against it, and fired his .38-caliber service revolver at Torresola, about 30 feet (10 m) away. Coffelt hit Torresola two inches above the ear, killing him instantly. Taken to the hospital, Coffelt died four hours later.

The gunfight involving Torresola lasted approximately 20 seconds, while the gunfight with Collazo lasted approximately 38.5 seconds. Only one of Collazo's shots hit anyone. Torresola did most of the shooting.

Aftermath

Coffelt's widow, Cressie E. Coffelt, was asked by President Truman and the Secretary of State to go to Puerto Rico, where she received condolences from various Puerto Rican leaders and crowds. Mrs. Coffelt responded with a speech absolving the island's people of blame for the acts of Collazo and Torresola.

Oscar Collazo was convicted in federal court and sentenced to death, which Truman commuted to a life sentence. While in prison, he gave an interview saying that his devotion to the Nationalist Party and Puerto Rican independence went back to 1932, when he had heard Pedro Albizu Campos give a speech about American imperialism and the outrage of American doctor Cornelius P. Rhoads writing about killing Puerto Ricans in experiments. (An investigation cleared the doctor of any crime.) In 1979, President Jimmy Carter commuted Collazo's sentence to the time served, and the former revolutionary was released. He returned to live in Puerto Rico, where he died in 1994.

At the time of the assassination attempt, the FBI arrested Collazo's wife, Rosa, on suspicion of having conspired with her husband in the plan. She spent eight months in federal prison but did not go to trial. Upon her release, Rosa continued to work with the Nationalist Party. She helped gather 100,000 signatures in an effort to save her husband from an execution.

Acknowledging the importance of the question of Puerto Rican independence, in 1952 Truman allowed a plebiscite in Puerto Rico to determine the status of its relationship to the U.S. The people voted 81.9% in favor of continuing as a Free Associated State, as established in 1950.

Gerald Ford assassination attempt in Sacramento

Gerald Ford assassination attempt in Sacramento

Ford being rushed by US Secret Service from 1975 Sacramento, California assassination attempt

Location	Capitol Park, south of 1121 L Street, Sacramento, California
Coordinates	38°34′29″N 121°29′21″WCoordinates: 38°34′29″N 121°29′21″W
Date	September 5, 1975 ~10:04 am (PST)
Target	Gerald Ford, 38th President of the United States
Attack type	Attempted political assassination via shooting

Weapon(s)	Colt M1911 .45 cal. semi-automatic pistol
Deaths	None
Injured (non-fatal)	None
Victim	President of the United States
Assailant	Lynette Fromme
Participant	One
Defender	Larry Buendorf, Secret Service agent
Motive	To set an example to those refusing to halt environmental pollution and its effects on Air, Trees, Water, and Animals (ATWA)

The Gerald Ford assassination attempt in Sacramento was a September 5, 1975, effort by Charles Manson Family cult member Lynette "Squeaky" Fromme to kill U.S. President Gerald Ford in California. She wanted to make a statement to people who refused to halt environmental pollution and its effects on Air, Trees, Water, and Animals (ATWA). Although Fromme stood a little more than an arm's length from Ford that Friday morning and pointed a M1911 pistol at him in the public grounds of the California State Capitol building, her gun failed to fire and no one was injured. After the assassination attempt, Ford continued walking to the California state house, where he met with California governor Jerry Brown. For her crime, Fromme spent 34 years in prison and was released on August 14, 2009 – 2 years and 8 months after Ford's death. The Gerald R. Ford Presidential Museum in Grand Rapids, Michigan, later received the M1911 pistol used in the assassination attempt as a gift, and the gun was put on display.

History

Lynette Alice Fromme, whose nickname "Squeaky" stemmed from her high-pitched voice, was a follower of cultist Charles Manson, leader of group convicted of murdering actress Sharon Tate and six others in Los Angeles, California in 1969 Fromme was one of the earliest, and had a reputation as being one of the most devoted, followers of Manson. Through the years, Fromme served as "the cornerstone" in keeping Manson cult members in communication with each other.

In April 1971, Fromme served 90 days in jail for attempting to feed a hamburger laced with the psychedelic drug LSD to Barbara Hoyt, a witness to the Tate murder, to keep Hoyt from testifying in the murder trial. Fromme moved to San Francisco to be closer to Manson in nearby San Quentin Prison. Later in 1972, she moved to Sacramento to maintain her proximity to Manson when he was transferred from San Quentin to Folsom Prison. In Sacramento, Fromme lived at 1725 P Street (38°34'16"N 121°29'09"W) in an attic apartment with Sandra Good, a close friend who also was a long-time member of the Manson Family. Three years later in 1975, Fromme decided to kill Ford to set an example for those refusing to halt environmental pollution and its effects on ATWA (Air, Trees, Water, Animals).

Events leading towards the assassination attempt

Ford's presidential daily diary for September 5, 1975

In July 1975, California's relatively new governor, Democrat Jerry Brown, had refused to commit to speak at the 49th annual Sacramento "Host Breakfast," an annual gathering of wealthy

California business leaders to be held in the Sacramento Convention Center on the morning of September 5, 1975. To teach Brown a political lesson for what he would describe more than 30 years later as a "dilatory response" to the invitation, the politically powerful group invited U.S. President Ford, a Republican, to make the September 5, 1975, morning speech instead. Ford saw California's electoral votes being critical to his success in the 1976 United States presidential election and accepted the invitation to speak at the Host Breakfast.

In early August 1975, *The New York Times* reported that United States Environmental Protection Agency had released a study entitled, "*A Spectroscopic Study of California Smog,*" showing that smog was widespread in rural areas. *The New York Times* article also noted how President Ford had just asked the United States Congress to relax provisions of the 1963 Clean Air Act beyond the 1970 Clean Air Act amendments and provided details on Ford's upcoming September trip to California. After learning of Ford's upcoming visit, ex-convict Thomas Elbert was arrested on August 18 in response to Elbert phoning the United States Secret Service and threatening to kill Ford when he visited Sacramento.

At about the same time, Fromme came to believe that California's giant coastal redwoods, the tallest trees in the world, were in danger of falling because of automobile smog reaching their rural location. Feeling personally responsible for the fate of the redwoods, Fromme traveled to San Francisco to meet with a San Francisco government official to save the trees from pollution. After returning from San Francisco, Fromme watched a news report from her P Street apartment and learned some details of Ford's plans to visit Sacramento. The hotel Ford would be staying at, the Senator Hotel, was located a little more than a one-half mile (0.80 km)—about fifteen minutes walking distance—from Fromme's Sacramento apartment. At this point, Fromme decided to bring attention to the trees by putting fear into the government through killing its symbol, President Ford.

How Fromme obtained the gun

On the day Fromme decided to see Ford during his September trip to Sacramento, Fromme already had a Colt .45 caliber semi-automatic pistol in her apartment. The M1911 pistol, produced 64 years earlier in 1911 by Colt Firearms, was manufactured the same year that Colt's M1911 pistol became the standard-issue side arm for the United States armed forces. After its manufacture in 1911, Fromme's pistol was sent to Rock Island Arsenal in Illinois. The pistol was used in the U.S. Army and later sold as Government surplus in

1913. At the time of the assassination attempt, the Colt .45 was not considered a common crime gun because "it's rather large, and not easily concealed."

Harold E. "Zeke"/"Manny" Boro, born 1909, was a retired federal government engineering draftsman who, at ages 65 to 66, hung around the Manson family and supplied them with money as a "sugar daddy".Boro met Fromme in the spring of 1974 while in a Sacramento park. Fromme would visit Boro at his apartment in Sacramento. In return for her friendship, Boro loaned his Cadillac to Fromme and later bought a red 1973 Volkswagen for her after she wrecked his Cadillac. On July 12, 1975, Boro moved from Sacramento to Jackson, California, at the end of Laughton Lane. While at his apartment in Jackson, Fromme asked Boro for a gun. Fromme told Boro that she needed one for her protection in the apartment house where she lived, with two roommates, due to enemies of Charles Manson. Boro had the pistol along with a half a box of ammunition, containing 25 rounds, and showed Fromme how to pull the hammer back and fire the pistol. Boro also had a pistol catalog in his apartment and allowed Fromme to look through it to select a different pistol for Boro to buy for Fromme. After that, Fromme walked out with the Colt .45, ammunition, and magazine, despite Boro's protest that she not take the pistol and other items.

Ford's activities the day before the assassination attempt

On September 4, 1975, the day before Fromme's assassination attempt in Sacramento, Ford was in Washington D.C. In the morning, he met with National Security Advisor and Secretary of State Henry Kissinger — a meeting that still was under national security restriction as of 2012. After the meeting, Ford flew the "Spirit of '76" from Andrews Air Force Base to Boeing Field in Seattle, Washington, to attend a Republican Party fund raising convention, tour the Fred Hutchinson Cancer Research Center, and attend a conference on domestic and economic affairs. At about 5:00 p.m., Ford then flew to Portland, Oregon, where he attended a Republican fundraising event, attended the Portland Youth Bicentennial Rally with about 13,000 children, and received an Oregon blanket gift. At 9:30 p.m., Ford flew to McClellan Air Force Base in Sacramento, California, and went to his suite at 11:30 p.m. at the Senator Hotel.

Assassination attempt

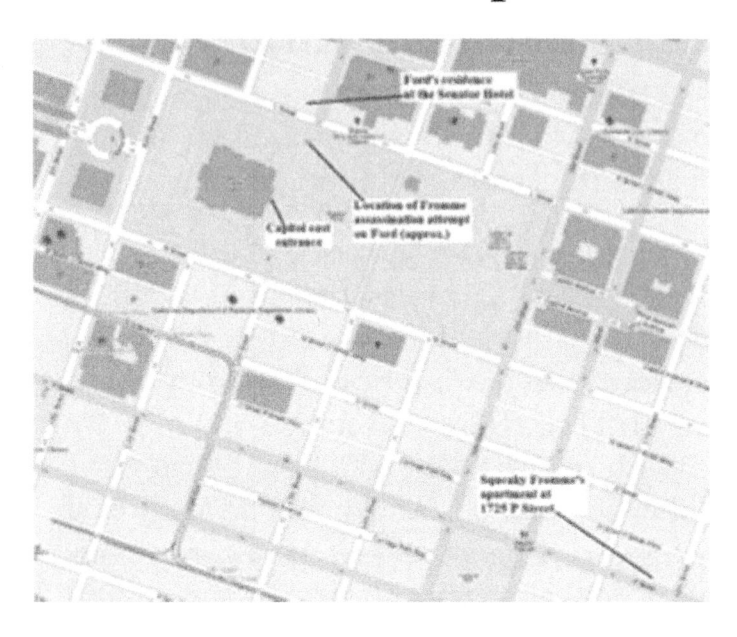

Ford assassination attempt in Sacramento location map

On the morning of September 5, 1975, Fromme dressed completely red "for the animals and earth colors," placed the Colt .45 pistol into a leg holster strapped to her left leg, and made her way from her apartment to the California state capitol grounds. The sky was clear and the weather prediction for Sacramento called for calm winds and a temperature around 84 °F (29 °C). At 9:26 a.m., Ford had returned to the Senator Hotel at 1121 L Street (38°34′39″N 121°29′31″W) from his two-hour speaking engagement at the Host Breakfast.

From his suite at the Senator Hotel, Ford crossed L Street, also known as Lincoln Highway, at 10:02 a.m. into Capitol Park and began shaking hands with people who had gathered in a crowd on the park's pathway. Ford was making his way toward an entrance of the state capitol building.

Ford had moved about 150 feet (46 m) from Lincoln Street along a Capitol Park paved walkway, saw "a woman in a brightly colored dress," and stopped approximately halfway to the state Capitol. People on either side of Ford wanted to shake hands with him and Ford assumed that the woman in red wanted to shake hands or talk. Twenty-six-year-old Fromme was positioned two feet (0.61 m) from Ford, behind the first row of the crowd, and reached into her flowing red robe, drawing the Colt .45 pistol from her leg holster. Fromme raised her right arm towards Ford, through the front row of people, and pointed the gun at a height between Ford's knees and his waist. From Ford's perspective, he noted, "... as I stopped, I saw a hand come through the crowd in the first row, and that was the first active gesture that I saw, but in the hand there was a gun."

The East Entrance of the California State Capitol looking north with the Hotel Senator in the background.

The pistol contained ammunition stored in a detachable magazine in the pistol's grip, but the gun did not include a round in the gun's chamber. At the time, Fromme was not aware that she needed to pull back the gun slide to insert a cartridge into the pistol's chamber. Five years later in 1980, from Federal Prison Camp, Alderson, Fromme claimed that she purposely ejected the top round from the pistol's magazine onto the floor of her P Street apartment, because she "was not determined to kill the guy."

Fromme's pistol, used in the September 5, 1975, Ford assassination attempt, on display at the Ford Presidential Museum

While Fromme pointed the gun at Ford, several people heard a "metallic click" sound. As the red-robed Fromme shouted, "It wouldn't go off", Secret Service agent Larry Buendorf grabbed the gun, forced it from Fromme's hand, and brought her to the ground. On the ground, Fromme said, "It didn't go off. Can you believe it? It didn't go off." One of the Secret Service agents shouted "get down, let's go." Secret Service agents then half-dragged Ford away from Fromme towards the east entrance of the Capitol, until Ford yelled in protest, "Put me down! Put me down!" Ford continued his walk to the California state house, entered, and then met with California governor Jerry Brown at

10:06 a.m. for 30 minutes without mentioning the assassination attempt until they were through talking business. Ford, who later indicated that he was not scared, concluded, "I thought I'd better get on with my day's schedule."

Aftermath

On September 20, 1975, United States federal judge Thomas J. MacBride set November 4, 1975 for the start of the trial against Fromme for attempting to assassinate a U.S. President. Three days before the trial began; President Ford gave a videotape testimony from the White House as a defense witness in the trial of Fromme. The testimony was the first time a U.S. President testified at a criminal trial.

On November 4, the prosecutors were ready to present about 1,000 items of evidence seized from Fromme's car and apartment just after the assassination attempt, including .45-caliber ammunition in the box she took from Boro and the book, *The Modern Handgun*. During the trial, Fromme refused to cooperate with her own defense, going so far as to throw an apple at prosecuting U.S. attorney Dwayne Keyes after he urged that Fromme's punishment be severe because she had shown herself to be "full of hate and violence".

Ford being greeted by his family at the White House in Washington D.C., about ten hours after the assassination attempt in California

The trial ended on November 19, 1975, with Fromme being convicted of attempting to assassinate President Ford. Fromme received a life sentence. During her imprisonment, Fromme escaped from prison and, as a result, received extra time to her sentence after her capture two days later, on December 26, 1987.

The Sacramento assassination attempt was the first assassination attempt against Ford during his presidency. On September 22, 1975, 17 days after Fromme attempted to kill Ford in Sacramento, Sara Jane Moore, a Patty Hearst fanatic, attempted to kill Ford in San Francisco. This second assassination attempt also failed and, two days later, California governor Jerry Brown responded to both assassination attempts on Ford's life in California by signing into law bills imposing mandatory sentences for persons convicted of using guns in committing serious crimes and requiring purchasers of guns to wait 15 days for delivery. Ford went on to complete his 1974–77 presidency without further assassination attempts.

In 1981, the Gerald R. Ford Presidential Museum was dedicated in Ford's hometown of Grand

Rapids, Michigan. On August 23, 1989, the Office of the United States Attorney in Sacramento donated Squeaky Fromme's pistol to the museum. Ford died of natural causes on December 26, 2006.

Fromme was released from prison on August 14, 2009, 2 years and 8 months after Ford's death and moved to Marcy, New York, to live in a house that "looks like an old metal Quonset hut from the World War II era" with Robert Valdner, who was released from prison in 1992 after killing his brother-in-law. As of 2012, the Ford Presidential Museum continued to maintain Squeaky Fromme's pistol on display next to a letter written by Sarah Jane Moore to Ford after she had been in prison for several months for attempting to kill him.

Attempted assassination of Ronald Reagan

Reagan assassination attempt	
Location	Washington, D.C.
Coordinates	38°54'58"N 77°02'43"W Coordinates: 38°54'58"N 77°02'43"W
Date	March 30, 1981 2:27 pm (Eastern Time)
Target	Ronald Reagan
Weapon(s)	Röhm RG-14 .22 cal.
Deaths	None
Injured (non-fatal)	4; James Brady, Timothy McCarthy, Thomas Delahanty, Ronald Reagan
Perpetrator	John Hinckley, Jr.

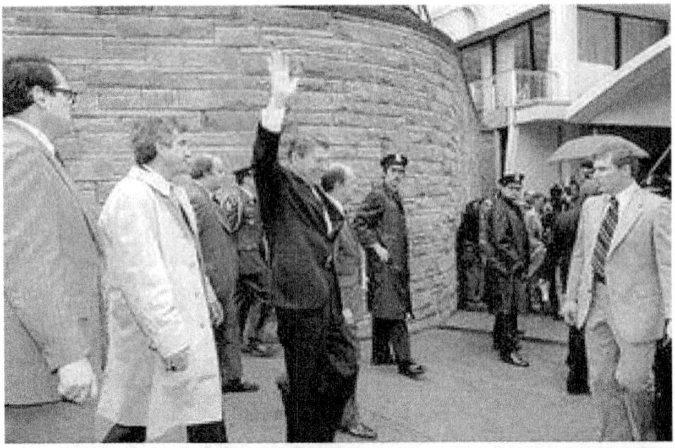

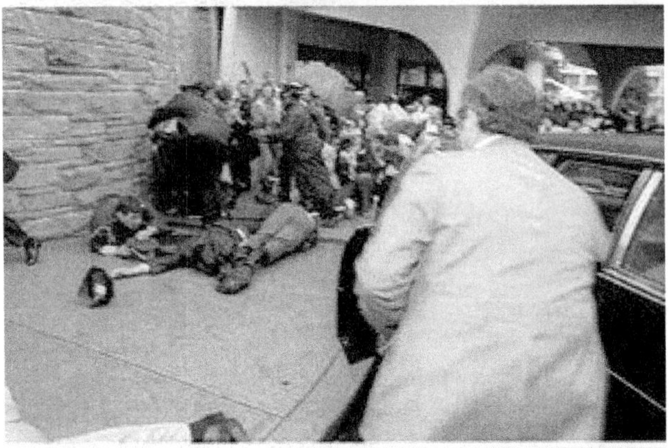

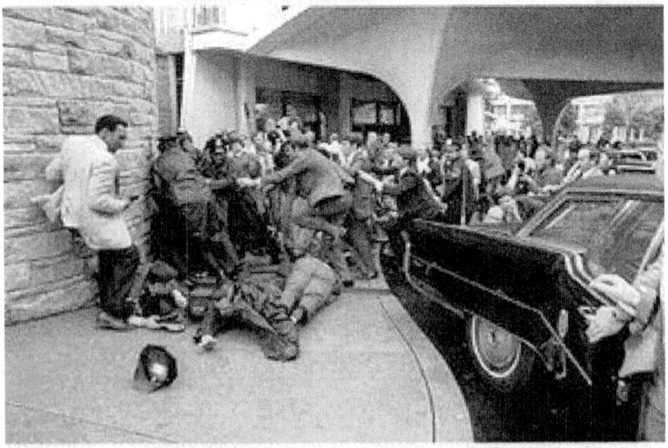

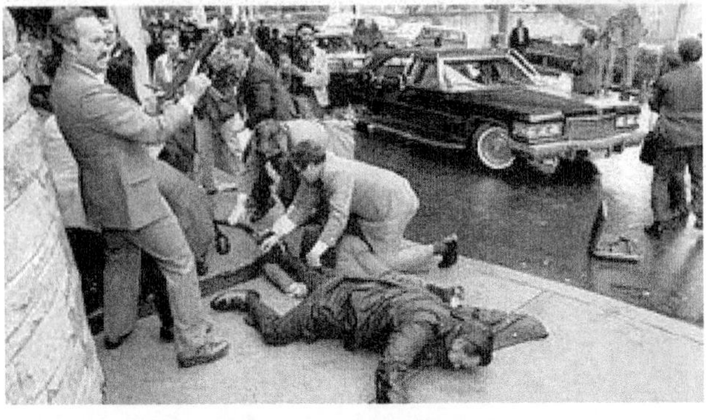

Secret Service Agent Robert Wanko can be seen in the last photo holding an Uzi.

The attempted assassination of Ronald Reagan occurred on Monday, March 30, 1981, 69 days into his presidency. While leaving a speaking engagement at the Washington Hilton Hotel in Washington, D.C., President Reagan and three others were shot and wounded by John Hinckley, Jr.

Reagan suffered a punctured lung and heavy internal bleeding, but prompt medical attention allowed him to recover quickly. Ronald Reagan was also shot in the chest and in the lower right arm. No formal invocation of presidential succession took place, although Secretary of State Alexander Haig controversially stated that he was "in control here" while Vice President George H. W. Bush returned to Washington.

Nobody was killed in the attack, though Press Secretary James Brady was left paralyzed and permanently disabled. Hinckley was found not guilty by reason of insanity and remains confined to a psychiatric facility.

Hinckley's motivation

Hinckley's motivation for the attack was born of his obsession with actress Jodie Foster due to erotomania. While living in Hollywood in the late 1970s, he saw the film *Taxi Driver* at least 15 times, apparently identifying strongly with Travis Bickle, the lead character portrayed by Robert De Niro. The arc of the story involves Bickle's attempts to protect a 12-year-old child prostitute, played by Foster. Towards the end of the film, Bickle attempts to assassinate a United States Senator who is running for president. Over the following years, Hinckley trailed Foster around the country, going so far as to enroll in a writing course at Yale University in 1980 after reading in *People* magazine that she was a student there. He wrote numerous letters and notes to her in late 1980. He called her twice and refused to give up when she indicated that she was not interested in him.

Convinced that by becoming a national figure he would be Foster's equal, Hinckley decided to emulate Bickle and began to stalk President Jimmy Carter. He was surprised at how easy it was to get close to the president—only one foot away at one event—but was arrested in October 1980 at Nashville International Airport for illegal possession of firearms; though Carter made a campaign stop there, the Federal Bureau of

Investigation did not connect this arrest to the President and did not notify the United States Secret Service. His parents briefly put him under the treatment of a psychiatrist. Subsequently, Hinckley turned his attention to Ronald Reagan whose election, he told his parents, would be good for the country. He wrote three or four more notes to Foster in early March 1981. Foster gave these notes to her dean, who gave them to the Yale police department, which sought to track Hinckley down but failed.

Assassination attempt

On March 21, 1981, Ronald Reagan, the new President of the United States, visited Ford's Theatre in Washington, D.C. with his wife Nancy for a fundraising event. He recalled, "I looked up at the presidential box above the stage where Abe Lincoln had been sitting the night he was shot and felt a curious sensation... I thought that even with all the Secret Service protection we now had, it was probably still possible for someone who had enough determination to get close enough to a president to shoot him."

Speaking engagement at the Washington Hilton Hotel

Hinckley arrived in Washington on Sunday, March 29, on a Greyhound Lines bus and checked into the Park Central Hotel. While eating breakfast at McDonald's the next morning, he noticed Reagan's schedule on page A4 of the *Washington Star*, and decided it was time to act. Knowing that he might not survive shooting the president, Hinckley wrote but did not mail a letter to Foster about two hours prior to the assassination attempt, saying that he hoped to impress her with the magnitude of his action and that he would "abandon the idea of getting Reagan in a second if I could only win your heart and live out the rest of my life with you."

On March 30, Reagan delivered a luncheon address to AFL-CIO representatives at the Washington Hilton Hotel. The hotel was considered the safest in Washington due to its secure, enclosed passageway called "President's Walk", built after the 1963 assassination of John F. Kennedy. Reagan entered the building through the passageway around 1:45, waving to a crowd of news media and citizens. While the Secret Service had made him wear a bulletproof vest for some events, Reagan did not wear one for the speech as his only public exposure would be the 30 feet between the hotel and his limousine, and the agency did not require vests for its agents that day. No one saw Hinckley behave in an unusual way; witnesses who reported him as "fidgety" and "agitated" apparently confused Hinckley with another person there that the Secret Service was monitoring.

Shooting

The Röhm RG-14 revolver at the Ronald Reagan Presidential Library.

At 2:27 pm Eastern Time, as Reagan exited the hotel through "President's Walk" and its T Street NW exit toward his waiting limousine, Hinckley waited within the crowd of admirers. While the Secret Service extensively screened those attending the president's speech, in a "colossal mistake" the agency allowed an unscreened group to stand within 15 ft (4.6 m) of him, behind a rope line. Unexpectedly, Reagan passed right in front of Hinckley. Believing he would never get a better chance, Hinckley fired a Röhm RG-14 .22 long rifle blue steel revolver six times in 1.7 seconds, missing the president with all six shots. The first bullet hit White House Press Secretary James Brady in the head. The second bullet hit District of Columbia police officer Thomas Delahanty in the back of his neck as he turned to protect Reagan. Hinckley now had a clear shot at the president, but the third bullet overshot him and hit the window of a building across the street. As Special Agent In Charge Jerry Parr quickly pushed Reagan into the limousine, the fourth bullet hit Secret Service agent Timothy McCarthy in the abdomen as he spread his body over Reagan to make himself a target. The fifth bullet hit the bullet-resistant glass of the window on the open side door of the limousine. The sixth and final bullet ricocheted off the armored side of the limousine and hit the president in his left underarm, grazing a rib and lodging in his lung, stopping nearly 1 inch (25mm) from his heart. Parr's prompt reaction saved Reagan from being hit in the head.

After the shooting, Alfred Antenucci, a Cleveland, Ohio, labor official who stood nearby Hinckley, was the first to respond. He saw the gun and hit Hinckley in the head, pulling the shooter down to the ground. Within two seconds agent Dennis McCarthy (no relation to agent Timothy McCarthy) dived onto the shooter as others threw him to the ground; intent on protecting Hinckley to avoid what happened to Lee Harvey Oswald, McCarthy had to "strike two citizens" to force them to release him. Agent Robert Wanko (misidentified as "Steve Wanko" in a newspaper report) took an Uzi from a briefcase to cover the President's evacuation and to deter a potential group attack.

Hinckley's gun was given to the ATF the day after the shooting to trace its origin. In just sixteen minutes agents found that the gun had been purchased at Rocky's Pawn Shop in Dallas, Texas. It had been loaded with six "Devastator"-brand cartridges which contained small aluminum and lead azide explosive charges designed to explode on contact; the bullet that hit Brady was the only one that exploded. On April 2, after learning that the others could explode at any time, volunteer doctors wearing bulletproof vests removed the bullet from Delahanty's neck.

George Washington University Hospital

After the Secret Service first announced "shots fired" over its radio network at 2:27 pm Reagan—

codename "Rawhide"—was taken away by the agents in the limousine ("Stagecoach"). At first, no one knew that he had been shot, and Parr stated that "Rawhide is OK...we're going to Crown" (the White House), as he preferred its medical facilities to an unsecured hospital.

In great pain from the bullet hitting a rib, the president believed that the rib had cracked when Parr pushed him into the limousine. When the agent checked him for gunshot wounds, however, Reagan coughed up bright, frothy blood. Although the president believed that he had cut his lip, Parr believed that the cracked rib had punctured Reagan's lung and ordered the motorcade to divert to nearby George Washington University Hospital, which the Secret Service periodically inspected for use. The limousine arrived there less than four minutes after leaving the hotel, while other agents took Hinckley to a District of Columbia jail, and Nancy Reagan ("Rainbow") left the White House for the hospital.

Although Parr had requested a stretcher, none were ready at the hospital, and it did not normally keep a stretcher at the emergency room's entrance. Reagan exited the limousine and insisted on walking. While he entered the hospital unassisted, once inside the president complained of difficulty breathing, his knees buckled, and he went down on one knee; Parr and others assisted him into the emergency room. The Physician to the President, Daniel Ruge, arrived with Reagan; believing that the president might have had a heart attack, he insisted that the hospital's trauma team, and not he himself or specialists from elsewhere, operate on him as it would treat any other patient. When a hospital employee asked Reagan aide Michael Deaver for the patient's name and address, only when Deaver stated "1600 Pennsylvania" did the worker realize that the President of the United States was in the emergency room.

The team, led by Joseph Giordano, cut off their patient's "thousand dollar" custom-made suit to examine him, angering Reagan. Military officers, including the one who carried the nuclear football, unsuccessfully tried to prevent FBI agents from confiscating the suit, Reagan's wallet, and other possessions as evidence; the Gold Codes card was in the wallet, and the FBI did not return it until two days later. The medical personnel found that Reagan's systolic blood pressure was 60 versus the normal 140, indicating that he was in shock, and knew that most 70-year-olds in the president's condition did not survive. Reagan was in excellent physical health, however, and also benefited from being shot by the .22 caliber instead of the larger .38. They treated him with intravenous fluids, oxygen, tetanus toxoid, and chest tubes, and surprised Parr—who still believed that he had cracked the president's rib—by finding the entrance gunshot wound. Brady and the wounded agent McCarthy were operated on near the president; when his wife arrived in the emergency room, Reagan remarked to her, "Honey, I forgot to duck", borrowing boxer Jack Dempsey's line to his wife the night he was beaten by Gene Tunney. While intubated, he scribbled to a nurse, "All in all, I'd rather be in Philadelphia", borrowing W. C. Fields' line. Although Reagan came close to death, the team's quick action—and Parr's decision to drive to the hospital instead of the White House—likely saved the president's life, and within 30 minutes Reagan left the emergency room for surgery with a normal blood pressure.

The chief of thoracic surgery, Benjamin L. Aaron, decided to perform a thoracotomy lasting 105 minutes because the bleeding persisted. Ultimately, Reagan lost over half of his blood volume in the emergency room and during surgery, which removed the bullet. In the operating room, Reagan removed his oxygen mask to joke, "I hope you are all Republicans." The doctors and nurses laughed, and Giordano, a liberal Democrat, replied, "Today, Mr. President, we are all Republicans." Reagan's post-operative course was complicated by fever, which was treated with multiple antibiotics. The surgery was routine enough that they predicted Reagan would be able to leave the hospital in two weeks and return to work at the Oval Office within a month.

"I am in control here"

A few days before the shooting, Vice President George H. W. Bush received the assignment of running crisis management in case of emergency despite Secretary of State Alexander Haig's objection. When the White House learned of the assassination attempt, however, Bush was over Texas aboard *Air Force Two*, which did not have secure voice communications, and his discussions with the White House were intercepted and given to the press. The vice president was notified in Fort Worth, Texas of the shooting within eight minutes, but relying on the initial reports that Reagan was unharmed his plane flew to Austin for a speech. After learning that the president was wounded, *Air Force Two* refueled in Austin before returning to Washington in what its pilot described as the fastest speed in the plane's history.

White House Counsel Fred Fielding immediately prepared for a transfer of presidential powers under the 25th Amendment, and Chief of Staff James A. Baker and Counselor to the President Edwin Meese went to Reagan's hospital still believing that the president was unharmed. Within five minutes of the shooting, members of the Cabinet began gathering in the White House Situation Room. Haig, Defense Secretary Caspar Weinberger, and National Security Advisor Richard Allen, discussed various issues, including the location of the nuclear football, the apparent presence of more than the usual number of Soviet submarines unusually close off the Atlantic coast, a possible Soviet invasion of Poland against the Solidarity movement, and the presidential line of succession. Although normally no tape recorders are allowed in the Situation Room these meetings were recorded with the participants' knowledge by Allen, and the tapes have since been made public.

The group obtained a duplicate nuclear football and Gold Codes card, and kept it in the situation room. (Reagan's football was still with the officer at the hospital, and Bush also had a card and football.) The participants discussed whether to raise the military's alert status, and the importance of doing so without changing the DEFCON level, although the number of Soviet submarines proved to be normal. Upon learning that Reagan was in surgery, Haig declared, "the helm is right here. And that means right in this chair for now, constitutionally, until the vice president gets here." The Secretary of State is not second in the line of succession but fourth, after the Vice President, Speaker of the House (Tip O'Neill), and the President *pro tempore* of the Senate (J. Strom Thurmond). O'Neill and Thurmond would have been required under 3 U.S.C. § 19 to resign their positions in order for either of them to become Acting President. Although others in the room knew that Haig's statement was constitutionally incorrect, they did not object at the time to avoid a confrontation.

Secretary of State Alexander Haig speaks to the press about the shooting.

At the same time, a press conference was underway in the White House. CBS reporter Lesley Stahl asked deputy press secretary Larry Speakes who was running the government, to which Speakes responded, "I cannot answer that question at this time." Upon hearing Speakes' remark, Haig scribbled out a note which was passed to Speakes, ordering him to leave the dais immediately. Moments later, Haig himself entered the briefing room, where he made the following controversial statement:

Constitutionally, gentlemen, you have the president, the vice president and the secretary of state, in that order, and should the president decide he wants to transfer the helm to the vice president, he will do so. As of now, I am in control here, in the White House, pending the return of the vice president and in close touch with him. If something came up, I would check with him, of course.

Those in the situation room reportedly laughed when they heard him say "I am in control here". Haig's statement reflected political reality, if not necessarily legal reality. He later said,

I wasn't talking about transition. I was talking about the executive branch, who is running the government. That was the question asked. It was not "Who is in line should the President die?"

Although Haig stated in the briefing room that "There are absolutely no alert measures that are necessary at this time or contemplated", while he spoke Weinberger raised the military's alert level. After Haig returned to the Situation Room, he objected to Weinberger doing so as it made him appear a liar. Weinberger and others accused Haig of exceeding his authority with his "I am in control" statement, while Haig defended himself by advising the others to "read the Constitution", saying that his comments did not involve "succession" and that he knew the "pecking order".

"Despite brief flare-ups and distractions," Allen recalled, "the crisis management team in the Situation Room worked well together. The congressional leadership was kept informed, and governments around the world were notified and reassured." Reagan's surgery ended at 6:20 pm, although he did not regain consciousness until 7:30 pm, so could not invoke Section 3 of the 25th Amendment to make Bush Acting President. The vice president arrived at the White House at 7:00 pm, and did not invoke Section 4 of the 25th Amendment. He stated on national television at 8:20 pm:

I can reassure this nation and a watching world that the American government is functioning fully and effectively. We've had full and complete communications throughout the day.

Public reaction

The assassination attempt was captured on video by several cameras, including those belonging to the Big Three television networks; ABC began airing footage at 2:42 pm. All three networks erroneously reported that Brady had died. While the Cable News Network (CNN) did not have a camera of its own at the shooting it was able to use

NBC's pool feed, and by staying on the story for 48 hours the network, less than a year old, built a reputation for thoroughness. Shocked Americans gathered around television sets in homes and shopping centers. Some cited the alleged Curse of Tippecanoe, and others recalled the assassinations of Kennedy and Martin Luther King, Jr. Newspapers printed extra editions and used gigantic headlines; the United States Senate adjourned, interrupting debate of Reagan's economic proposals; and churches held prayer services.

Hinckley asked the arresting officers whether that night's Academy Awards ceremony would be postponed due to the shooting and it was; the ceremony—for which former actor Reagan had taped a message—occurred the next evening. Because the president survived surgery with a good prognosis, the 1981 NCAA Men's Division I Basketball Tournament championship game that day was not postponed, although the audience of 18,000 in Philadelphia held a moment of silence before the game. The Dow Jones Industrial Average declined due to the shooting before the New York Stock Exchange closed early, but the index rose the next day as Reagan recovered. Beyond having to postpone its Academy Awards broadcast, ABC temporarily renamed the lead character of *The Greatest American Hero* from "Ralph Hinkley" to "Hanley", and NBC postponed a forthcoming episode of *Walking Tall* titled "Hit Man".

Aftermath

The Reagans wave from the White House after President Reagan's return from the hospital on April 11. Reagan wore a bulletproof vest under his red sweater.

Reagan was the first serving U.S. President to survive being shot in an assassination attempt. The members of his staff were anxious for the president to appear to be recovering quickly, and the morning after his operation he saw visitors and signed a piece of legislation. Reagan left the hospital on the 13th day. Initially, he worked two hours a day in the White House's residential quarters, with meetings held there instead of the Oval Office. Reagan did not lead a Cabinet meeting until day 26, did not leave Washington until day 49, and did not hold a press conference until day 79. Ruge thought recovery was not complete until October. Reagan's plans for the month after the shooting were canceled, including a visit to the Mission Control Center at Lyndon B. Johnson Space Center in Houston, Texas, in April 1981 during STS-1, the first flight of the Space Shuttle. Vice President Bush instead called the orbiting astronauts during their mission. Reagan would visit Mission Control during STS-2 that November.

The attempt had great influence on Reagan's popularity; polls indicated his approval rating to be around 73%. Reagan believed that God had spared his life so that he might go on to fulfill a greater purpose and, although not a Catholic, meetings with Mother Teresa, Cardinal Terence Cooke, and fellow shooting survivor Pope John Paul II reinforced this belief. Agent Parr came to believe that God had directed his life to save Reagan, and became a pastor.

Reagan returned to the Oval Office on April 25, receiving a standing ovation from staff and Cabinet members; referring to their teamwork in his absence, he insisted, "I should be applauding you." His first public appearance was an April 28 speech before the joint houses of Congress to introduce his planned spending cuts, a campaign promise. He received "two thunderous standing ovations", which the *New York Times* deemed "a salute to his good health" as well as his programs, which the president introduced using a medical recovery theme. Reagan installed a gym in the White House and began regularly exercising there; gaining so much muscle that he had to buy new suits. The shooting caused Nancy Reagan to be afraid for her husband's safety, however. She asked him to not run for reelection in 1984, and due to her fears began consulting astrologer Joan Quigley.

The two law enforcement officers recovered from their wounds, although Delahanty was forced to retire due to his injuries. The attack seriously wounded the President's Press Secretary, James Brady, who sustained a serious head wound and became permanently disabled. Brady remained as Press Secretary for the remainder of Reagan's administration, but this was primarily a titular role. Later, Brady and his wife Sarah became leading advocates of gun control and other actions to reduce the amount of gun violence in the United States. They also became active in the lobbying organization Handgun Control, Inc. – which would eventually be renamed the Brady Campaign to Prevent Gun Violence – and founded the non-profit Brady Center to Prevent Gun Violence. The

Brady Handgun Violence Prevention Act was passed in 1993 as a result of their work.

The shooting of Reagan widened a debate on gun control in the U.S. that the death of John Lennon in December 1980 had started. Reagan expressed opposition to increased handgun control following Lennon's death and re-iterated his opposition after his own shooting. However in a speech at an event marking the assassination attempt's 10th anniversary, Reagan endorsed the Brady Act:

"Anniversary" is a word we usually associate with happy events that we like to remember: birthdays, weddings, and the first job. March 30, however, marks an anniversary I would just as soon forget, but cannot... four lives were changed forever, and all by a Saturday-night special – a cheaply made .22 caliber pistol – purchased in a Dallas pawnshop by a young man with a history of mental disturbance. This nightmare might never have happened if legislation that is before Congress now – the Brady bill – had been law back in 1981... If the passage of the Brady bill were to result in a reduction of only 10 or 15 percent of those numbers (and it could be a good deal greater), it would be well worth making it the law of the land. And there would be a lot fewer families facing anniversaries such as the Bradys, Delahantys, McCarthys and Reagans face every March 30.

James Brady in August 2006

Hinckley was found not guilty by reason of insanity on June 21, 1982. The defense psychiatric reports had found him to be insane while the prosecution reports declared him legally sane. Following his lawyers' advice, he declined to take the stand in his own defense. Hinckley was confined at St. Elizabeths Hospital in Washington, D.C., where he is still being held. After his trial, he wrote that the shooting was "the greatest love offering in the history of the world", and did not indicate any regrets.

The not-guilty verdict led to widespread dismay, and, as a result, the U.S. Congress and a number of states rewrote laws regarding the insanity defense. The old Model Penal Code test was replaced by a test that shifts the burden of proof regarding a defendant's sanity from the prosecution to the defendant. Three states have abolished the defense altogether.

Jodie Foster was hounded relentlessly by the media in early 1981 because she was Hinckley's target of obsession. Since then, Foster has only commented on Hinckley on three occasions: a press conference a few days after the attack, an article she wrote in 1982, and during an interview with Charlie Rose on *60 Minutes II* in 1999; she has otherwise ended or canceled several interviews after the event was mentioned or if the interviewer was going to bring up Hinckley.

The "President's Walk," the unenclosed outer door from which Reagan had left the hotel shortly before being shot, was altered subsequent to the assassination attempt. The open canopy above the door was removed and a brick drive-through enclosure was constructed to allow the president to move directly from the door of his car into the hotel without public access.

During the 2010-2011 renovation done in preparation for the celebration of the one-hundredth anniversary of his birth, the Ronald Reagan Presidential Library and Museum in Simi Valley, California, installed a sound and photo diorama depicting the assassination attempt, and visitors are warned of startling gunshot effects.

Alfred Antenucci almost had a heart attack and was hospitalized soon after the shooting. He had a private meeting with Reagan, who gave him cufflinks with the Presidential Seal and a Presidential Honor, and his hometown of Garfield Heights, Ohio, named a street Antenucci Boulevard. In 1984, Antenucci died of a heart attack in his home. The Garfield Heights Historical Society has the cufflinks on display.

Printed in Great Britain
by Amazon